C. Wood Davis

A Compendium of the World's Food Production and

Consumption

C. Wood Davis

A Compendium of the World's Food Production and Consumption

ISBN/EAN: 9783744646123

Printed in Europe, USA, Canada, Australia, Japan

Cover: Foto ©Andreas Hilbeck / pixelio.de

More available books at **www.hansebooks.com**

A COMPENDIUM

OF THE WORLD'S

Food Production and Consumption

The Railway · The Market Wrecker.

— BY —

C. WOOD DAVIS.

AUTHOR OF VARIOUS PAPERS IN THE ' FORUM," "ARENA" AND OTHER PERIODICALS.

The thanks of the Public and the Author are due to the many Foreign Officials and American Ministers and Consuls who have courteously aided in collecting the official data embraced in these pages, and which gives them such value as they may possess.

PUBLISHED BY THE AUTHOR,

GODDARD, KANSAS, U. S. A.

EAGLE PRINTING HOUSE, WICHITA, KANSAS.

(In preparation and will issue in 1892.)

"THE FOOD SUPPLY."

PRESENT AND FUTURE.

— BY —

C. WOOD DAVIS.

In which will be reviewed the condition of Agriculture in each (separately) of the grain-growing countries, official data being tabulated (for each) showing, for a series of recent years, the acreage devoted to the production of each of the food staples as well as the production, consumption, exportation and importation of each staple product and the per capita requirements ; the design being to include all the food-bearing areas contributing, materially, to the subsistence of the bread-eating peoples with the hope that the work can be so thoroughly done as to render the book of value to all classes and desirable for reference. To this will be appended such of the papers of the Author, heretofore published, as appear to have permanent value.

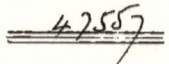

"A KANSAS RANCH,"

— BY —

MARIE M. AND C. WOOD DAVIS.

A ROMANCE OF EARLY KANSAS DAYS,

AND SHOWING THE METHODS OF RAILWAY MANIPULATION AND WHO WERE THE MANIPULATORS,

Is in preparation, and will appear early in 1892.

FOOD AND POPULATION.

Since 1870 food has, relatively to population, been more abundant and procurable at a less expenditure of labor than at any time in the history of the race, and the absence of war and the abundance and cheapness of the means of subsistence have, among the industrial classes, stimulated marriage with the result of unprecedented additions to the populations of European blood and the enthusiast, without over-much reflection, has assumed that humanity was entering upon an age when neither war, want nor scarcity would be known. It is, however, very questionable if this view of the situation is tenable, and investigations—begun some years since by the writer—the results of which are now embodied in tabulations of official data, as to the relative rates of increase of the consuming populations and the productive power (as shown by the acreage at the close of the 7th, 8th and 9th decades) of the fields of the temperate zones render it more than doubtful as to any prolongation of this period of abundance and cheapness.

That the treatment of this question may partake as little as possible of the speculative and explore only that future, where probable conditions may reasonably be assumed from those now existant, it is the purpose to limit the period under review to the eighth and ninth decades of the nineteenth century and extend the prevision no farther than the close of the first decade of the twentieth.

Such limitation of the retrospective is rendered necessary by the fact that agricultural statistics are of such recent growth that "looking backward" beyond 1870 would be venturing into a realm where no reliable data exists.

Under the designations of "bread-eating populations" and "bread-eaters" are included only the peoples of Europe, the United States, British America, the Cape regions of South Africa, Australasia, South America south of the tropics, and the colonial European populations of the islands and tropical regions, the geographical distribution having been as follows at the close of the last three decades:

	1870	1880	1890
Europe	303 000,000	329,000,000	368 000,000
United States	38,600,000	50,200,000	62 500,000
Canada	3,600,000	4,300,000	5,300,000
Australasia	2,000,000	2,900 000	4,200,000
Temperate South America	5,000 000	6,600,000	8,200,000
South Africa and Islands	6,800,000	7,000,000	7,800,000
Totals	359,000,000	400,000,000	456 000,000

For the reasons stated the aggregate increase of the bread-eating populations and the rate of increase, during the eighth decade, were greater than ever before known, necessitating the opening of new sources of food supply, such sources having been mostly found upon the fertile plains of North America and in newly developed Indian exports and the supplies from these sources increased so rapidly that in the latter part of the decade they became excessive, as is clear from the descending scale of prices then obtaining and the fact that the per capita quota of land in wheat increased from .427 of an acre in 1870 to .443 of an acre in 1880 and this apparently trifling addition—aggregating, however, 6 400,000 acres—to the acreage quota resulted in unusual abundance, great reduction in the cost of bread and all primary food staples and a proportionate lowering of the returns of cultivator and landlord and showing with what certainty, and to what degree, even so trifling a disturbance of the exact and delicate relations existing between production and consumption will affect the price of those things which render civilized life possible.

The cheapening of the means of subsistence and accompanying peace has, in Europe, been followed by an increase in the relative number of marriages and births and at the same time cheap and more abundant nourishment, coupled with better sanitary conditions, have added to the average duration of life, the result being that the bread-eaters of the world increased, during the eighth decade at the rate of 11.4 per cent., while the means of subsistence, as measured by the area devoted to the production of grain and potatoes, increased 12 5 per cent., as set forth in the following table:

THE WORLD'S AREA IN FOOD STAPLES.

Products.	1870 Acres.	1880 Acres.	1890 Acres.	20 Yrs Incr'se and Decrease in Acres	20 Yrs. Incr'se and Decrease per cent.
Wheat	153,362,000	177,310,000	181,474 000	28,112,000*	11.5*
Rye	109,076,000	108,345,000	108,364,000	712,000†	.7†
Barley	45,386,000	43,480,000	44,650,000	736,000†	1.6†
Oats	78,700,000	90,903 000	104,888,000	26,188,000*	33 3*
Maize, etc	84,178,000	110,377,000	127,832,000	43,654,000*	52.0*
Potatoes	21,765,000	23,616,000	25,839.000	4.074,000*	18.7*
Totals	492,467,000	554,031,000	593 047,000	100,580,000‡	20.4‡

* Indicates Increase and † decrease.   ‡Net Increase.

In twenty years we find an increase of 20.4 per cent. in the aggregate acreage of all food staples as against an increase of 27 per cent. in the bread-eating populations and taking into consideration only the two principal bread-making grains—wheat and rye—the increase has been but 10.4 per cent., from which it appears that during the twenty years the bread-eaters have increased more than two and a half times as fast as the mate rial from which bread is made.

During the eighth decade, however, the wheat acreage increased 15.6 per cent. as against an increase in the consuming element of 11.4 per cent. and the result was an excessive production of wheat, a part of which was consumed to make up for the diminishing production of rye and the remainder accumulated as a reserve which has sufficed to tide over later years, when both acreage and current production have been less than current needs.

During the earlier years of the ninth decade the acreage in food staples continued to increase more rapidly than population, although the rate of such increase was progressively lessening, and about the middle of the decade fell in the rear of the population rate, which progressed from the 11.4 per cent. of the eighth decade to 14 per cent., the aggregate increase being 56,000,000 as against 41,000,000 of the preceding ten years.

From the foregoing tables it appears that while population has, by peace and an abundant supply of the cheapest food ever known, been stimulated to such an increase the area devoted to staple food crops has of late, ceased to expand in like proportion and the acreage, relatively to population, has shrunken to less than that of the earlier years of the eighth decade, when the bread-making grains bore a price 85 per cent. higher than that obtaining in 1890.

At the close of the eighth decade the per capita quota of land in wheat was .443 of an acre, but at the close of the ninth decade the bread-eaters had so increased that the acreage of wheat, upon which each unit of the population could draw, had diminished to .398 of an acre, being seven per cent. less than the .427 of an acre quota of 1870, when the price was 85 per cent. higher. The reasons for this abnormal condition of the supply, as related to the exceptionally low prices prevailing from 1884 to 1890 inclusive, are to be found in that the world's wheat acreage (as measured by the area per capita in cultivation during the earlier years of the eighth decade when prices were such as to indicate that the supply was neither over-abundant nor deficient) was excessive in 1880 by some 6,400 000 and had been excessive for some years prior thereto and so continued up to about the middle of the ninth decade, such excess gradually disappearing—as population increased without a proportionate increase in wheat acreage—and consumption overtaking current production, such production has since been deficient with the exception of years when, as in 1887, the yield has been much above the average.

During the existence of an excessive acreage accumulations of bread-stuffs—large in the aggregate—were made in mill, warehouse and farm granary, the world over, and in the years of excessive area the product of one harvest over-lapped the succeeding one in such a way that even two such short (world) crops as those of 1885 and 1886 had no effect in advancing prices, although they were—respectively—50,000,000 and 93,000,000 bushels below the average. Indeed, the price continued to fall, the average (gold) price per bushel for the year (in England) dropping from $1.07 in 1884 to 99 cents in 1885, and then to 94 cents in 1886. On the other hand, when accumulations have been exhausted, as after the world, in the harvest of 1890, had garnered a crop 50,000 000 bushels above the average; so great has been the growth of population, so small the increase af acreage and product and so complete the exhaustion of the reserves that the price at which the great crop of 1890 has been sold will average 25 per cent greater than that received for the deficient one of 1889, which was 137 000 000 bushels less but was supplemented by the residue of the reserves accumulated in the earlier part of the ninth decade and from the great crop of 1887, which was the largest ever produced.

From the best data obtainable the world appears to have produced, during each of the past ten years, the quantity of wheat stated in the following table:

YEAR	BUSHELS OF WHEAT	YEAR	BUSHELS OF WHEAT
1881	1,977 000 000	1886	2 043,000,000
1882	2,263 000,000	1887	2,267,000,000
1883	2,059,000 000	1888	2,183 000,000
1884	2,263,000,000	1889	2 048,000,000
1885	2,077,000,000	1890	2,185,000,000

Yearly average, 1881 to 1885 inclusive............2,126,000,000 bushels
"   "   1886 to 1890   "   ....2 145,000,000 bushels
"   "   for the decade.............. ....2,136,000,000 bushels

While in the eighth decade the relative increase in wheat acreage and population was as four is to three the increase in the ninth was in the inverse ratio of one to six.

In the eighth decade the per capita quota of land in wheat increased 3.8 per cent., yet in the ninth it diminished 10.2 per cent. and is now 7 per cent. less than in 1870.

During the eighth decade the area in all food staples—exclusive of the United States —increased but 9,375,000 acres, being 2.2 per cent., as against an increase in the bread-eating populations—also exclusive of the United States—of 29,400,000, or 9.2 per cent., the ratio being as one is to four and a half.

During the ninth decade the area in all food staples—exclusive of the United States —increased but 9,011,000 acres, being 2 per cent., as against an increase in the bread-eating populations—also exclusive of the United States—of 43,700,000, or 11.1 per cent., the ratio being as one is to five and a half.

During the twenty years from 1870 to 1890 the area in staple food products in the temperate zones—exclusive of the United States—increased but 18 386,000 acres, being 4.4 per cent., as against an increase in the bread-eaters—also exclusive of the United States— of 73,100,000 or 22.8 per cent., the ratio being as one is to five.

Including the acreage and population of the United States the world's increase of area under the staple food crops of the temperate zones has during the last twenty years, been 100,580 000 acres and the rate of increase 20.4 per cent. as against an increase in the bread-eating populations of 27 per cent., the ratio being as three is to four. The aggregates and percentages of such increase and the acreage quota of each unit of the bread-eating populations at the end of each of three decennial periods have been as shown in the following table:

Year	Bread-Eating Populations	Increase Per Cent.	World's Area in Food Staples	Aggregate Increase in Acres	Increase Per Cent.	Acreage Quota Per Capita
1870	359,000,000	......	492,167,000	....	......	1.37
1880	400,000,000	11.4	554,031,000	61,564,000	12.5	1.39
1890	456,000,000	14.0	593,047,000	39,016,000	7.0	1.30
20 yrs. increase		27.0	....	100,580,000	20.4	......

The increase in acreage, during the eighth decade, was one-tenth greater than the increase in population and the result low prices for farm products and a great shrinkage in land values the world over.

During the ninth decade, on the contrary, population increased at a rate double that obtaining as to acreage in food staples, the result now being an ascending scale of prices for farm products, an advance in land values, coming scarcity and a very brisk demand for farm products.

A most significant fact, made very clear by the forgoing table, is that with a seventh more people to feed the increase in the acreage devoted to food production, during the ninth decade, was but a little more than half what it was in the eighth, when to have kept pace with the increase in population it should have been 36 per cent. greater and there can be no reasonable doubt that but for the acreage in excess of current needs, existing at the beginning of the ninth decade, the pinch of scarcity would long since have been felt.

It is equally significant that the United States has contributed such a very large proportion to of all recent additions to the world's food producing areas, the extent and proportions of such contributions being made clear in the subjoined table, where is shown the aggregate of all such additions, the number of acres contributed by the United States and the percentage of the whole so contributed:

Year	World's Area in Food Staples	Total Acres Add'd to Area in Food St'pl's	Acres C'ntrib'ted by United States	Percentage C'ntrib'ted by United States
1870...	492.467,000	....	....	......
1880.........	554 031.000	61,564,000	52.189,000	84.7
18.0..	593,047,000	39.016 000	29,945,000	77.0
20 years increase..........................	....	100,580,000	82 134,000	81.7

This and the preceding tables show that during the last twenty years the consuming population has increased one-third faster than the products to be consumed but this disproportionate increase has all occurred in the ninth decade (and the greater part of it within the last five years), as in the eighth decade the increase in acreage was 12.5 per cent. as against an increase in population of 11.4 per cent., while in the ninth the propor. tions have been an increase of 14 per cent. in the consuming element and but 7 per cent. in the area devoted to all food staples.

Of the 100,580,000 acres added to the world's food producing area it is shown in the last table that no less than 82,000,000. or nearly 82 per cent., must be credited to the United States and during the 15 years ending with 1885 our additions were quite equal to the entire added requirements of the world. Since 1885, however, our additions to the area in staple crops has been less than half that required to meet the increasing needs of our own population, hence we have found it necessary to draw the needed supplies from the acreage heretofore employed in producing food for exportation and the 21,000,000 acres so employed in 1885 has now been reduced, by augmenting domestic needs, to 10,000,000 and as we shall at no remote day. require the entire product of our fields, we may well ask when will such conditions obtain, how will the world then fare for food and whence can Europe hope to draw the needed supplies?

In dealing with these problems bread-stuffs will, as in the commercial and agricultural world, be treated as the controlling factor and for this purpose wheat and rye should be considered as one.

Of the two principal bread-making grains rye constitutes about 38 per cent. and enters in the proportion of 47 per cent. into the bread consumed in Europe.

The wheat area of the world, any part of the product of which finds its way into the channels of commerce, has, during the last decade, produced crops averaging 2,136,-000,000 bushels per annum, the average for the five years ending with 1885 being 2,126,-000,000 as against 2,145,000,000 bushels during the last five years, this increase of 19,000,000 bushels being in accord with an increase in area found to be less than 2,000 000 acres although in the meantime the added requirements of the added bread-eaters have been such that the producing area, to have kept pace with such needs, should have increased not less than 13,000,000 acres, and there was a small acreage deficit as early as 1885 and the re-quirements are now such that an average yield, from every acre in the world devoted to wheat culture, would give a product fully 100.000.000 bushels less than current needs, and this deficit, growing out of an acreage 10,000,000 to 12,000 000 acres too small for the world's requirements, is augmenting at the rate of more than 2,000,000 acres yearly, and will so long as the additions to the world's wheat area are, as of late years, less than 400,000 acres per annum.

There also exists a very great deficit in the rye acreage, the extent of which it is difficult to measure, as during the period when wheat was over-abundant and rye growing relatively scarce wheat was largely substituted for the deficient rye (as is now being done in Germany and Russia), but we get some idea of this deficit when we ascertain that in 1870, when the per capita quota for the world's bread-eaters was .427 of an acre of wheat, that of rye was .304 of an acre and is now reduced to .238 of an acre, the per capita quota of wheat and rye then being .731 of an acre as against .636 of an acre in 1890, the reduction in the per capita acreage—as compared with that of the early part of the eighth decade—of the two grains being .095 of an acre, or 13 per cent., and indicating a shortage of 43,000,000 acres unless in the meantime other forms of food have been substituted for the deficient wheat and rye, and such has doubtless been the case to some extent in Russia, and possibly other countries, where maize, millet and other cheap forms have been substituted, but such substitutions can not have been considerable, as European production of no one of the food staples has kept pace with the increase of European population, as is clear from the following table, showing European acreages in the various staples at the end the last three decennial periods and the aggregates and percentages of increase and decrease:

Products	1870 Acres	1880 Acres	1890 Acres	Increase and Decrease Acres.	Increase and Decrease Per Cent.
Wheat and Spelt‡	93,989,624	93,190,754	94,445,613	455,989*	.49*
Rye and Maslin‡	107,827,389	106,440,143	105,876,411	1,950,958†	1.81†
Barley	39,392,899	36,380,668	36,009,809	3,383,090†	8.58†
Oats	68,008,422	71,417,938	73,608,435	5,600,013*	8.24*
Maize, etc	42,682,017	44,244,679	43,928,806	1,246,678*	2.92*
Potatoes	19,947,017	21,196,381	22,664,761	2,717,744*	13.50*
Totals	371,847,368	372,870,563	376,533,835		
Twenty years net increase				4,686,000*	1.25*

* Indicates increase and † decrease. ‡Spelt is a variety of wheat and maslin is rye and wheat sown trgether.

It may be assumed that, for some time, the bread-eating populations will—unless food becomes exceedingly scarce and high—increase nearly as fast as during the ninth decade, but to be clearly on the safe side, the increase, during the remainder of the century, will be estimated at 11 per cent. and for the ensuing ten years at 10 per cent., and estimat. ing that the per capita requirements will equal those of the earlier years of the eighth decade, when the price of bread-stuffs was 85 per cent. greater than in 1890, population and additional acreage requirements for 1900 and 1910 are estimated at the numbers stated in the following table:

Year	Estimated Bread-Eating Population	Additional Acres Wheat Required	Additional Acres Rye Required	Additional Acres Other Staples Required	Total Additional Acres Required
1900	506 000.000	21,000 000	15,000,000	32 000,000	68,000,000
1910	556,000,900	21,000,000	15,000,000	32,000,000	68,000.000
Totals		42 000 000	30,000,000	64 000 000	136,000,000

Granting the substantial correctness of the preceding estimate, it follows that the world must, within ten years, add 68,000,000 acres to the food producing areas of the temperate zones, or reduce the standard of living in the same ratio as the added acreage falls short of the requirements, and must add many—30 to 40—millions to make good the ex. isting deficit in wheat and rye areas. In the next decade another 68,000,000 acres must be added, hence it is safe to say that during the next twenty years the additions to the acreage must be two-thirds greater than during the last twenty, and such additions, if we are to continue the present standard of living, can not be less tha 166,000,000 acres.

Where is it possible to find such a quantity of available land with the populations necessary to its cultivation?

When we reflect that the basis from which we now start to add to the consuming population is 27 per cent. greater than twenty years since and that this population is, by reason of its greater volume and the long prevalence of peace, increasing, in the aggre. gate, twice as fast as it did thirty years ago, that the augmentation during the coming twenty years will be a half greater than the present population of the United States, that their requirements for food are increasing in like ratio and that the available lands are daily becoming less abundant, the task before the generation becomes more plain and its difficulties such as to address themselves to the thoughtful attention of those who have been entrusted with the direction of public affairs, and it were well to take careful ac. count of the world's resources.

Some will suggest that Providence will care for our welfare and see that the children of men do not want, while others will advance the theory that the acreage under cultiva. tion can, by better methods, be made to produce much more; some euthuastic writers placing the increment from better methods at 100 per cent., but they are evidently not aware that changing meteorological conditions are the controlling factors in agricultural production, nor can they be very well acquainted with the characteristics of the cultivat. ing class who, time out of mind, have been proverbial for the reluctance with which they change processes handed down from father to son. While it is probable that additions to the acreage yield will result from the adoption of better methods of culture and fertiliza. tion, yet the improvement in this direction is likely to be so slow as to be hardly apprecia ble with the passage of a limited number of years.

Others believe that such improved methods will no more than maintain the existing fertility of the cultivated lands, contending that its original fertility is being rapidly dis. sipated and instance in proof of such contention the diminishing production of American fields, as shown in the reports of the Department of Agriculture, and such argument is not without weight, if but the face of the returns is looked at, as they show average yields per acre as follows:

Products	Average yield per Acre 8th Decade in Bushels	Average yield per Acre 9th Decade in Bushels	Percentages of Decrease
Corn	27.1	24.1	12.5
Wheat	12.4	12.1	2.5
Oats	28.4	26.6	6.8
Barley	22.0	21.7	1.4
Rye	14.1	11.9	15.6
Buckwheat	17.7	12.8	27.6

While there has clearly been a reduction in the acreage yield due to diminishing fertility, or the bringing under cultivation of lands of lower productive power, this show. ing is deceptive in as much as the acreage in all crops was, each year of the eighth decade, greatly understated by the Department, as was made manifest by the census of 1880, when the departmental returns were found to be some 26,000 000 acres less than the census count, and such under-estimate necessarily increased the reported product per acre and these errors, exceed, except in the case of rye, the last ten years' reduction in acreage yield, thus vitiating all arguments based upon the diminishing yield shown by the Depart. mental reports without rendering it necessary to resort to the explanation, advanced by the Departmental statistician, that the diminishing yield was due to a succession of un. favorable seasons.

The writer believes that the increased production which will result from the adop tion of better methods of culture, in suburban and other favorably located districts, will no more than compensate for the lessening yield of more remote districts and the con. stant addition of acres of lower average fertility.

Continued cultivation will lessen the productive power of the soil where the means or incentive for fertilization are lacking, and this is as true of India as of the United States, as lands that, in the reign of Akbar, gave an average yield of 19 bushels of wheat per acre now yield but 14, the reduction being more than 26 per cent. and due to continued use without proper fertilization.

An increase in production, due to better methods, will come so slowly as to be of little avail in relieving necessities that will soon be very pressing and to meet the requirements of the near-by years we must depend largely upon an extension of the cultivated area, hence it is pertinent to enquire where exist available lands, what are their extent, and can the bread-eating world rely upon development keeping pace with increasing requirements?

Aside from lands that may be brought into use for pasturage the writer has—in the *Forum* for June, 1890, and elswhere—estimated that possibly 35,000,000 acres will, within twenty years, be added to the area in the United States devoted to the production of staples, and while officials, employed to enquire into the extent of the irrigable lands of the arid districts, express the opinion that a great part of the arid areas can be profitably irrigated, yet their estimates are so extravagant as to be unworthy a moment's consideration by one familiar with the arid regions, one such estimate being that 200,000,000 acres of these wastes are susceptible of irrigation. The utter recklessness of such an estimate will be instantly apparent to one who has seen much of the arid area when he reflects that such areas embrace less than 800,000,000 acres and that this estimate contemplates the reclamation of one acre out of four, when it is very doubtful if one acre in thirty can be irrigated.

If there are 35,000,000 acres which can, after providing for the pasturage of a due proportion of horses, cattle and sheep, be, within twenty years, brought under the plow and devoted to the production of food staples our population will have so increased as to require the product of every such acre, as well as the 10,000,000 now employed in the production of food for exportation, as each year's addition to the population will be 1,500,000 or more and consume the product of 4,500,000 acres, and if we are to continue the exportation of tobacco and cotton, in anything like present proportions, it will be necessary to add nearly 5,000 000 new acres annually to the plowed fields, and this is more than double the area now being added if the reports of the Agricultural Department are any criterion.

Many suppose that when wheat becomes scarce it will only be necessary to divert enough of the meadows and corn fields to its production to meet the increased requirements, but it would be impossible to conceive a more fallacious idea, as there exists a very close and delicate relationship between population, consumption and production, and the moment the proportions of this relationship are disturbed, either by a change in the ratio of acreage, a reduction or increase of average acreage yield, by reason of more or less favorable meteorological conditions, or an exacting foreign demand, that moment prices will oscillate as have those of corn, oats and wheat during the last two years.

As, for several previous years, the corn acreage of 1889 was much in excess of domestic requirements, and the season being exceptionably favorable. the per capita supply was nearly 35 bushels against requirements—domestic and foreign—of something less than 30 bushels, and the result was a large surplus with prices sinking to the lowest level known since the civil war.

In 1890 climatic conditions were the reverse of those of the previous year and the aggregate out-turn of corn a fourth less, the result being scarcity, high prices and the sending to the shambles of hecatombs of half-grown cattle and swine that the farmer lacked the corn to fatten.

The relationship between supply and demand is accurately, if unconciously, adjusted by the farmer as he devotes his land to such products as bring the best returns and when the area in any staple is reduced below the needs of the population just so soon the price of such product will become relatively higher than that by which it has been displaced, hence when a staple so important as wheat becomes scarce and high in price so will advance the price of all staples; otherwise all the land would gravitate to the production of the more profitable one, and yet, while the farmer adjusts his crops to meet a growing or lessening demand for the various staples. the short seller of the Board of Trade fixes the price a' which such products shall be sold.

The writer is not aware that until within two years an attempt had ever been made to determine the proportion of land required in each staple for the subsistence of a given number of people and was led to make tentative computations of acreage requirements per capita for the purpose of ascertaining what relation the domestic consumption of each staple bore to the total of land under cultivation, as well as to determine how soon the area employed in the production of food for exportation would be required to supply food for home needs, and has been able to ascertain from the total production during the ninth decade—less the quantities exported—that the yearly requirements per capita for domestic consumption have been the product of 1.19 acres of corn, .48 of an acre of wheat, .39 of an acre of oats, .64 of an acre of hay, .11 of an acre of cotton and .15 of an acre in rye, barley, buckwheat, potatoes and tobacco (to which should be added .20 of an acre for the cotton exported), and such acreage ratios can not be disturbed without affecting prices; except as relates to such products as are produced in excess of domestic requirements, and then the price will be subject to change as the relationship of such product, to the whole bread-eating population, is affected by the world's supply, largely irrespective of the local supply, as has so often been the case with wheat.

If, by diverting land to wheat, we should reduce the corn area below 1.19 acres per capita the price of corn would advance, and should such diversion proceed far, or be long continued, the price of corn would become relatively much higher than that for wheat, as is now the case in Argentina, where the corn crop having failed wheat and maize are being sold at the same price per bushel, when the parity of prices is about two and a half to one.

Having a surplus acreage in corn and the world's very deficient wheat acreage assuring a very high price for that grain, it would be wise to divert two or three million acres of the corn land to wheat for a year or so and thus greatly advance the price of corn, but such land must revert to corn not later than 1893 or 1894 as increasing requirements are such as to absorb the product of 1,800,000 additional acres of corn each year and the surplus corn area is now less than 2,000,000 acres.

When this surplus acreage has been absorbed we must yearly trench upon the wheat fields for the needed additions to the corn area, as there is but little new corn land to be brought under cultivation and wheat is the only staple, other than corn and cotton, of which there is an acreage the product of which is exported, and we shall certainly supply home needs before attempting to furnish Europe with either bread or meat.

Of 39,000,000 acres in wheat 1,000,000 have, within a year, been taken from the corn area, and, as in 1895, we shall, for domestic consumption, require the product of but about 34,000,000 acres in wheat and needing to add 1,800,000 acres per year to the corn area, it would appear that to furnish the needed corn we must, before 1896, have taken from the wheat area the 5,000,000 surplus acres, hence it does not seem likely that we can export any part of the staple products of our fields after 1895 except cotton and tobacco.

Part of the wheat acreage must be thus diverted or the domestic consumption of all the other staples be reduced, as the additions to the acreage are so far from meeting the requirements of current additions to the population that the entire acreage now producing food for export will have been absorbed by domestic consumption within five years, hence it follows that the exportation of food must then cease or we must lower the standard of living.

That the arable areas of Europe are very fully occupied is made manifest in the table showing European crop acreages, and while some increase of the cultivated area may be expected in Eastern Europe, it is not likely to more than keep pace with local requirements. Other than this any material expansion is improbable. Nor can the meadows and other fields be diverted to wheat production without causing a scarcity of products quite as necessary and which have been displacing wheat in Western Europe, as wheat would better bear carriage and could be more readily procured from abroad.

In South America are large areas adapted to cereal culture, of which less than 5,000,000 acres are employed in growing wheat, and about the same area in other crops, the whole of temperate South America having less land in cultivation than has Nebraska, and this region will have made quite as much progress as can be expected if the cultivated area shall have been doubled by 1910, as the social, political, fiscal and industrial conditions are such as to ensure tardy development. This region, however, has the distinction of being the only one where the area devoted to wheat has during the ninth decade, increased faster than domestic requirements.

Australasia contains much good wheat land, a small part of which has been brought into use, but since 1880 the area in wheat has not increased as rapidly as domestic needs, the acreage, relatively to population, having diminished nearly five per cent. and the total area under cultivation still more.

Insufficient population and deficient means of transportation preclude a rapid extension of the Australasian wheat area, but the most potent cause of retardation will probably be found in long term pastoral leases which cover vast tracts of the most desirable lands, which can not be opened for cultivation until these leases expire, hence there is little reason to expect much increase of wheat exportation from Australasia during this century.

We get a clear conception of the relative importance of Australasian agriculture when we remember that the total area under cereals and potatoes, in all the seven colonies, is but 5,190,000 acres and is but 37 per cent. of the area devoted to such crops in the State of Illinois, and the cultivated area of the whole southern hemisphere, outside of the tropics, is less than that of the one State named.

The cereal contributions of India cannot increase and are likely to diminish rapidly, as the population is increasing more than one per cent. per annum while the area under cultivation increases not one-third as fast and is not capable of much expansion while the agricultural population, other than that of Bengal (where the Indian government has not the power to increase the land tax owing to a permanent settlement had in 1793), are constantly in a state of semi-starvation.

The Indian wheat area has shown no increase in twenty years, and there are thoughtful citizens of India who anticipate the early cessation of exports from the necessity of devoting the entire product of the fields to the subsistence of a population increasing about 3,000,000 yearly, and that requires, even at the miserable Indian standard of living, the addition of nearly 2,000,000 new acres per annum.

The political, social and industrial conditions environing the populations of Algeria, Tunis and Morocco preclude any material expansion of wheat culture in Northern Africa at an early day and similar conditions obtaining in the Asiatic dependencies of Turkey, no considerable additions to the wheat supply may be looked for in that direction, while in Egypt the culture of wheat is being slowly displaced by that of sugar, cotton and the cheaper foods required by an augmenting population.

Siberia and Northwestern Canada remain as sources of possible supply, yet neither possesses the requisite population for an early increase of wheat production on a scale at all commensurate with the world's pressing needs.

There seems no doubt, however, that in Siberia is an immense area suited to colonization and the production of cereals, but political and social conditions, as well as the tenure of the land, are such as to render it quite probable that it will not soon become an outlet for the swarming European populations, other than those of Russia and the development will be so slow as to afford little hope as to the supplies from this source being of the required volume.

It is contended that there exists in Northwestern Canada an extensive region adapted to the profitable culture of cereals. While the fertility of much of this region is unquestionable it is practically unoccupied, without the means of transportation and its adaptation to wheat culture still but hypothetical, as there has been, over the most of this wide area, no such continued culture as to dispel reasonable doubts (arising from its geographical situation) as to the summer heats being ordinarily sufficient to ripen wheat. But for this doubt we might say that, when occupied, Northwestern Canada would add materially to the world's supply of bread, but existing conditions, as to population and transportation, are such that no material relief from the scarcity now impending, by reason of the existing and prospective deficient wheat and rye acreage of the world, can be hoped for from this source as time is such an important element in the problem. A hungry man can not wait for his breakfast until an unoccupied region can be peopled and its lands subdued, and to-day the world is not only short in bread-stuff by reason of deficient acreage, but the great disaster which has befallen the growing crops of Europe, coupled with the deficient acreage, render it reasonably certain that the yield of the world's wheat and rye fields in 1891 will be less than current needs by hundreds of millions of bushels and that the last vestige of the reserves, accumulated during the existence of a surplus acreage, will have disappeared and an unpleasant void still remain, and this condition should ensure very high prices for our products, and once the pinch is felt in consequence of the exhaustion of the reserves, prices should, and will, remain high while the acreage deficit exists, and that it will long exist is assured by the scarcity of available lands in the termperate zones.

THE EXHAUSTION OF THE ARABLE LANDS.

Nearly twenty years since, Gen. W. B. Hazen pointed out the approaching exhaustion of the arable lands of the United States, and was sharply criticised for certain statements as to the aridity and unfitness for agriculture of the lands west of the 100th meridian. Time and repeated attempts to subject such lands to cultivation have shown the correctness of Gen. Hazen's statements and conclusions. A little more than a score of years since, Iowa, Missouri, Kansas, Nebraska and the Dakotas constituted a vast district but sparsely settled, the area then in cultivation in those States being but little more than seven million acres; now, however, by the opening of new farms and the development of older ones, the area in staple crops (in such States) is much more than one-fourth of all the lands in the United States so employed. With such an area of the most fertile soils in the process of development it is not strange that Gen. Hazen's views were looked upon as pessimistic; yet their correctness can no longer be questioned.

The writer has recently shown that the existing depression in agriculture is due, in part, to an excessive development of these fertile districts; that agriculture and all related industries can be prosperous only when consumption balances production; and that an early equilibration is assured by the growing scarcity of tillable lands. Investigations, undertaken solely with the view of ascertaining why the farmer was not prosperous, led irresistably to the conclusion that the rapid increase of the cultivated area in the United States was one of the causes of the lack of prosperity among the farmers of Canada and Europe, as well as of the United States, and that the great reduction in the yearly accretions to such cultivated acreage was a sure presage of the early coming of the time when the farmer will be prosperous. Further investigations have developed the fact that the arable lands are being occupied at a rate which insures their complete exhaustion at a much earlier date than has heretofore been deemed possible, with rapid reduction in the volume of exportable breadstuffs, and an entire and not remote cessation of such exports, probably to be followed by our entering the markets of the world for a portion of the wheat required for domestic consumption.

To understand the situation clearly, it is best to resort to tabular statements showing the increase in cultivated acres in different districts during designated periods, the rate of increase in each district in such periods, the aggregate of the additions to the cultivated acreage in each period, the yearly average of such additions for each period, the percentages of such increase for each period as well as the yearly average of such percentages, and a comparison of the periodical rate of increase of acreage with that of population. This is shown in the following table:

†Groups of States.	Surface Area of Each Group	Cultivated Area in Staple Crops 1867	In Staple Crops 1874	Percentages of Decrease and Increase 1867 to 1874	In Staple Crops 1879	Percentages of Increase 1874 to 1879	In Staple Crops 1884	Percentages of Increase 1879 to 1884	In Staple Crops 1889	Percentages of Increase 1884 to 1889
North Atlantic	117,063,680	24,290,679	20,095,201	*17.0−	25,300,000	25.8	25,381,221	0.3	25,812,000	1.7
Lake	206,784,669	31,331,211	37,277,419	19.0	47,054,210	26.2	52,912,402	12.4	56,207,000	6.6
Missouri valley	274,069,251	7,429,928	18,668,861	151.3	34,369,967	84.1	49,953,764	45.3	56,012,000	12.1
Southern	522,194,948	29,125,249	33,340,163	14.5	48,561,259	45.6	58,119,953	19.7	62,957,000	8.3
Mountain States and Territories	553,047,040	286,459	272,876	2.2	1,250,000	32.7	1,519,973	21.6	2,150,000	41.4
Pacific coast	206,764,160	1,970,000	3,738,244	89.8	4,505,876	20.6	7,362,306	63.3	7,861,000	6.8
Indian Territory	41,481,600									
Totals in cultivation		94,343,526	113,412,764	20.2	161,041,312	42.0	196,249,619	21.2	211,000,000	6.1
Increase of cultivated acres each period, and rate per cent. of such increase			19,069,238	20.2	47,628,548	42.0	34,208,307	21.2	15,750,351	6.1
Population and per-centage of increase during each period		36,211,000	42,796,000	18.2	48,886,000	14.2	55,000,000	12.1	61,100,000	11.1
Average annual increase of cultivated acres each period, and yearly rate per cent of such increase			2,724,177	2.9	9,525,710	8.4	6,841,661	4.2	3,150,276	1.6

†"North Atlantic"—Seaboard States from Maine to Maryland, and Vermont.
"Lake"—Ohio, Indiana, Illinois, Michigan, Wisconsin and Minnesota.
"Missouri Valley"—Iowa, Missouri, Kansas, Nebraska and the Dakotas.
"Southern"—all south of the Potomac and Ohio, and Arkansas and Texas.
"Pacific Coast"—California, Oregon and Washington.
"Mountain States and Territories"—all else except the Indian Territory, Alaska and public land strip.

The preceding exhibit, covering twenty-two years of greatest expansion in American agriculture, is divided into four periods, the first being seven years and each of the others five. In the seven-year period, population is found to have increased 18.2 per cent. and the cultivated area 20.2 per cent.; the drafts upon the arable lands, in the shape of additions to the acreage in staple crops, amounting to 2,724,177 acres per annum, and aggregating 19,069,238 acres. During the second peroid—five years—population increased 14.2 per cent. and the area in cultivation 42 per cent., the average annual additions to the cultivated area being no less than 9,525,710 acres, and aggregating 47,628.548 acres. The third period shows population increasing a trifle more than 12 per cent., cultivated acres 21.2 per cent., and an average annual addition to the area in staple crops of 6,841,661 acres; the aggregate reaching 34,208,307, which was still out of proportion to the increase in population. During the five years ending in 1889, the rate at which population increased was somewhat less than in the preceding periods, but the rate of increase in cultivated acres was reduced to 8.1 per cent., being but 1.6 per cent. per annum; the average annual increment of the cultivated area shringing to 3,150,276 acres—little more than half the normal requirements—and clearly showing the rapid diminution of the arable lands.

Although the population was 12,200,000 greater in 1889 than ten years earlier, and the desire for farms just as keen as ever, yet in the last five years, with fully a fourth more people desirous of becoming owners of farms, the number of acres added to the cultivated area was but one-third as great as during the five years ending in 1879; being in the latter period 15,750,000 acres, as against 47,628,000 acres iu the earlier one; whereas, had the increase in acreage been in the same ratio to population as in the earlier period, such additions would have reached a total of 60,000,000 acres. The land hunger being quite as sharp now as in the eighth decade, it is evident that there is a lack of the means of gratifying it.

The foregoing table and the partial analysis following enable us to see the progress of agricultural development and the occupation and gradual diminution of the arable areas in the several districts. They help to a clearer appreciation of the effects of such rapid development upon the agricultural and other interests, and indicate plainly that the existing depression is, in part, due to an increase in cultivated acres out of all proportion to the synchronous increase in population, at the same time suggesting the inquiry: Where can be found the arable lands to satisfy the land-hungry home-seekers now ready to settle, in countless swarms, upon any fraction of an Indian reservation that is at all likely to be thrown open to settlement?

The unoccupied area in the North Atlantic group covers some 7,500,000 acres. It lies mostly in the Aroostook and Adirondack regions, and is almost wholly unfit for cultivation being either rough and mountainous, swampy, or heavily timbered, with soils of very low fertility, of which but a small fraction can be brought under cultivation. In Michigan, Wisconsin and Minnesota are tracts aggregating some 10 000,000 acres which are valuable only for the forest growths above and the minerals below the surface. These lands will add but little to the cultivated acreage.

Such portions of Texas, Kansas, Nebraska and the Dakotas as lie west of the 100th meridian have generally been included among the arable areas, and it has been esteemed an act of treason for a citizen of any one of those States to maintain that only such parts of this vast tract as are susceptible of irrigation can rightfully be so designated. This immense plains area, covering as well large parts of New Mexico, Colorado, Wyoming and Montana, is at best but a pastoral region, in which repeated attempts have been made to reduce the lands to cultivation. Successive armies of settlers have invaded these desiccated plains, but after expending their means and suffering deplorable hardships, have found it necessary to abandon land and improvements. This is the area from which arises that perennial cry for aid, as it is also the land from which a refluent wave of population moves eastward with as much regularity as the return of Autumn.

Much of the soil being fairly fertile, these plains offer no obstacles to settlement and cultivation, except such as are found in the climate; that presents the same peculiarities of aridity, extreme variations in temperature and excessive evaporation found in the elevated regions of Central Asia. It is true that near the eastern borders of this tract fine crops are occasionally grown, but only in years when the rainfall is exceptionally great and the dreaded simoom fails to wither vegetation. Such exceptional seasons, however, are but "a snare and a delusion," inducing men to waste their energies and means in abortive attempts to cultivate these arid soils. Occasionally the arid features of the climate of the plains are projected several degrees eastward, sometimes reaching Missouri and Arkansas, with disastrous results to the husbandman.

Could water for irrigation be obtained, much of the plains region could be made productive; but most of the streams penetrating it are even now yearly drained dry by irrigating canals, which supply water to irrigate but the smallest fraction of these immense areas During the seasons of 1887, 1888, 1889 and 1890 (and nearly every year of late), many miles of such canals remained dry during the entire Summer, owing to the complete appropriation of the water by canals opening from such streams nearer their source. In seasons of excessive drouth and deficient snowfall the water available is lessened one-half or more; hence irrigation from the water flowing in such streams has about reached its limit. This is notably true of the Platte, Arkansas, Cimarron and Rio Grande.

Many schemes have been proposed for utilizing the water said to flow below the sand in the valleys, but such projects involve immense outlays, are as yet unfruitful, and, it is generally believed, will long remain so. Should such plans, however, ultimately prove successful, the resulting supply would suffice to irrigate but an inconsiderable fraction of the arid lands, being rarely applicable outside the immediate vicinity of the streams.

Extending from the Gulf to far north of the Canadian boundary, and from the vicinity of the 100th meridian to the Rocky Mountains, the plains embrace an area of hundreds of millions of acres, of which probably one-fourth, with sufficient water for irrigation, could be made productive; but under existing conditions it is very doubtful if three per cent. should be included under the term arable, and such arable part is nearly or quite all occupied, even though a part of it is unimproved.

Lying west of the plains is the still more arid region of the mountain ranges and plateaus, where are found numerous fertile valleys, mostly of limited extent, which, when not at too great an elevation, and when supplied with water for irrigation, are very productive; yet in such favored localities occur seasons of excessive drouth, when the supply of water (resulting mostly from melting snow) proves wholly inadequate for the limited acreage under cultivation, as was the case in Nevada, Utah, and other arid districts in 1887, 1888, 1889 and 1890.

The regions where irrigation is a condition precedent to successful agriculture include an area of some 784,000,000 acres, of which, owing to scarcity of water and lack of soil, not more than five per cent. is susceptible of cultivation; and there is no satisfactory evidence that water can be obtained to irrigate the half of five per cent. The construction of extensive irrigation works necessitates the expenditure of much money and takes long periods of time, and few of those now living will see the completion of such works as will be required to irrigate the 30,000,000 acres of arid lands which the Public Land Commission estimates as irrigable from existing supplies of water.

In adopting the estimate of the Public Land Commission, that but 30,000,000 acres of the arid lands are irrigable from the available supply of water, I am not unmindful of the fact that such estimate conflicts with that recently made public by Major Powell* (who was a member of the Public Land Commission) namely, that "there are nearly 1,000,-000,000 acres of these arid lands in the United States, of which nearly 120,000,000 acres can be irrigated when all such waters are used."

I am unable to accept such an estimate for many reasons, one of which is found in the fact that the arid areas include something less than 800,000,000 acres, or less than 80 per cent of the 1,000,000,000 acres named by Major Powell.

Nearly or quite all those familiar with the arid regions consider the estimate of the Commission, that one acre in twenty is susceptible of irrigation, quite as high as the facts warrant; and it should be borne in mind that most of the arid lands which could be easily and cheaply irrigated have already been brought under the plow, yet less than one per cent. of the area is in cultivation.

Before any considerable additions can be made to the irrigated lands extensive

*"Century Magazine." March, 1890.

surveys* must be made; existing claims, water rights, and titles—inchoate and complete —extinguished; national and State laws formulated and enacted that will harmonize or extinguish conflicting national, State, municipal, corporate and individual interests; and then extensive and costly works constructed—all of which will consume much time. In the interim, population and consumption will have outrun production, the small remainder of the unoccupied non-irrigable arable lands will have disappeared, and such portions of the arid districts as can be brought under the plow will be needed to meet the urgent wants of an ever increasing consuming element.

The processes and progress of agricultural development in prairie regions where rains are ordinarily sufficient, and in mountain districts where arable lands, susceptible of irrigation, exist only in tracts of small extent, differ most radically, as is evident when the progress made in Nebraska and Kansas is contrasted with that made in Colorado and Utah. Utah has been settled more than forty years; Colorado, Nebraska and, Kansas from thirty to thirty-five years. In 1888, Colorado had 520,000 acres employed in growing staple crops; Utah, 396,000; Nebraska, 8,141,000; and Kansas 10,552,000; the cultivated area in Kansas being twelve times that of Colorado and Utah. Had any considerable part of the lands of the mountain districts been arable and susceptible of irrigation. they would long since have been seized upon for farms by the great army of the landless.

The uncultivable character of the lands of plain and mountain districts, and the rapid diminution of the unoccupied arable soils of the United States, have been clearly shown by the events following the opening to settlement of the limited and not over-fertile Oklahoma country, when men who had failed to find satisfactory locations in California, Oregon and Washington retraced their steps, hoping to secure land upon which to found a home, only to find in advance of them an army of would-be settlers large enough to occupy a territory ten times the size of Oklahoma. Similar scenes have more recently been enacted upon the opening of a part of the Sioux reservation, where a land-hungry myriad, in the depth of a Dakota Winter, contended for the possession of lands wholly within the belt where the farmer must strive with drouth and a soil below the average in fertility.

While I write, an army of settlers is camped along the southern Kansas border, impatiently waiting a proclamation from the President—which may not come for many months—opening to settlement the good, bad and indifferent lands of the Cherokee Outlet; which body of land will probably furnish some 20,000 fair to good farms of 160 acres each, and a like number that will not pay for cultivation; the remaining 16,000 quarter sections being fit only for pasturage, and much of it of little worth for that purpose. These statements will not be chalenged by those familiar with that country, unless they are engaged in "booming" the district in question.

In California, as well as in the States of the Missouri valley, there is much land yet unoccupied, mostly in the possession of corporations and individuals who are holding it for Henry George's "unearned increment." These lands are likely to be brought into cultivation very tardily, and in such a manner as to add but little to the area in grain crops, as they will no more than replace lands diverted from cereal culture to pasture and meadow—a diversion necessitated by the constantly increasing number of animals kept.

In Oregon and Washington are great unoccupied areas. Such portions of these unoccupied lands as lie east of the Cascade Mountains—say two-thirds of each State— possess many of the characteristics of other mountain districts. Such small portions of western Oregon and Washington as are without timber have long been occupied, while the remainder of these fertile districts is so heavily timbered as to render such lands unavailable as a source of food supply during this century.

Far at the southeast, in Florida, is found an immense unoccupied area—some 12,-000,000 acres or more—but this region is a land of sand-barrens, impassible swamps, dense forests and everglades, little of which is fit for human habitation. Long as Florida has been settled, and though by reason of possessing the advantages of a semi-tropical climate it has become the Winter abode of so many well-to-do people, it shows but little agricult-

---

*Major Powell proposes four different surveys topographic, hydrographic, engineering and geological—which will certainly require several decades to complete. and which will cost vast sums.

ural development. doubtless because of the sterility and uncultivable character of a great part of the lands. The result is that, aside from the area employed in growing fruits and vegetables, less than three per cent. of the surface of the State is in cultivation. With such a showing, it is clear that Florida will make no material additions, at an early day, to the area employed in growing staple crops.

Scattered through the southern States are many unoccupied tracts; but of these only a small part can be designated as arable, for much of such land is swamp, mountain or subject to overflow; this being especially true of such remnants of the public domain as are still to be found in the southern districts. Still we are likely to see some extension of the cultivated area in southern States, more especially in Arkansas and Texas; there being in those States much unimproved land included in farms which will hereafter be reduced to cultivation and used, largely, to augment the world's supply of cotton.

In the Indian Territory is found the only large body of fairly fertile lands yet to be brought into cultivation. The area of that Territory is 44,481,000 acres, the eastern two-thirds of which possess a soil of average fertility, while the remainder is much below the average. The peculiar climatic conditions of the arid plains are frequently projected over the western portion, rendering mixed farming but a precarious means of subsistence. Various tracts in the Territory will be opened to settlement from time to time as the Indian titles are extinguished; but it will be mostly in the western and by far the poorer part, for the eastern and better soils will for a long time remain in the possession of the Indians and "squaw men." The Indian and his white son-in-law and tenant now cultivate much land possibly 500,000 to 1,000,000 acres), of which, as early as 1880, a large proportion was in cotton. Within the last year, 16,000 bales of cotton were shipped from one station. Although the products of the Indian Territory, for reasons known only to the Departmental barnacles, are not included in the reports of the Department of Agriculture, yet they enter into consumption and make some additions to the marketable surplus; and this acreage will in time appear in the reports probably as current additions to the area in staple crops.

The foregoing table and text afford a reasonable basis for an estimate of the lands that can be added to the cultivated area within a given period, say during this decade. But before proceeding to make such estimate, it may be well to inquire what the Public Land Commission had to say on this subject in its report for 1880, wherein it was estimated, June 30, 1879 "that (exclusive of certain lands in the southern States) of lands over which the survey and disposition laws had been extended, lying in the West, the United States did not own, of arable agricultural lands which could be cultivated without irrigation or other artificial appliances, more than the area of the State of Ohio, viz: 25,000,000 acres "

"Of the public domain then remaining the Commission made the following estimate:

Timber lands............	85,000 000 acres.
Coal lands (to be largely increased by better classification)..............	5,520,000 "
Mineral lands (subject to a large increase by new discoveries)..............	64,800,000 "
Arable lands in northern States and Territories............	17,800,000 "
Lands in southern States surveyed and unsurveyed............	25,589 000 "
Irrigable lands, being the lands which can be irrigated from the present supply of water............	30,000 000 "
The remainder. pasturage, grazing, desert and all other lands useless for agricultural purpos – s by reason of altitude or lack of water or soil, including remainder of lands likely to be segregated for private land grants still unsatisfied, and Indian and military reservations, including also unsurveyed area of the Indian Territory, viz: 17,150,250 acres............	565,701,222 " "

An analysis of this estimate will show that of the public domain unoccupied in 1880, there were then some 100 000,000 acres which might be included under the designation arable, and made up as follows:

17,800,000	acres	of arable lands in northern States and Territories.
7,000,000	"	in southern States.
30,000 000	"	of irrigable lands.
17,000,000	"	in Indian Territory.
28,000,000	"	of surrendered railway grants, and Indian and military reservations.

100,800,000 acres total.

Since 1880, more than 60,000,000 acres of these lands have been occupied and largely brought into use, and the only unoccupied remainder of any moment is found in the lands of the Indian Territory, and in that portion of the widely scattered irrigable lands yet unsettled, the available total of which cannot exceed 40,000,000 acres, and is probably much less; and these lands are so conditioned that development must be slow. To these 40,000,000 acres may be added an indefinite quantity of railway, school, college and State lands, much of which is wholly unfit for cultivation. Estimating with extreme liberality, the arable portion of these lands may be put at 30,000,000 acres; then, adding 30,000,000 acres more as the undeveloped arable lands now constituting parts of farms, or yet unoccupied lands owned by individuals, we have a possible total of 100,000,000 acres yet to be brought into use, equivalent to 650,000 farms of 160 acres each.

Of the farm areas included in the census of 1880, thirty-five per cent. was in woodland, thirty-one per cent was employed in growing staple crops, and the remainder was in minor crops, or reckoned as farm yards, pasturage and unused waste land. It is probable that the proportion employed in growing staple crops has risen to one-third; and we may assume that thirty-five per cent. will be the maximum proportion of the new farm areas added from the possible 100,000,000 acres that will be devoted to the production of staple crops, thus increasing the productive power some 16.6 per cent. Such increase is likely to be less, rather than more than one-sixth, for no inconsiderable part of these lands is even now included in farms, and will come under the plow very slowly, if at all oeing now largely in use for grazing farm animals; and the requirements for that purpose are constantly increasing. It is also well to remember that 100,000,000 acres, the available arable area still remaining, is the sum of estimates liberal in the extreme, and that in New Mexico and Arizona alleged Spanish and Mexican grants are likely for a long time to retard development. According to the ascertained per capita requirements the existing cultivated area is sufficient for nearly 67,000,000 people, and with an addition of one-sixth we have a potential supply of cultivated acres sufficient for a population of 77,000,000. which number will probably be reached in 1900 with an annual increase of but 2.2 per cent.; but not till many years after 1900 will all these lands be brought into production. Could 35 per cent. of 100,000,000 acres be at once reduced to cultivation, the added acreage in staple crops would barely furnish supplies for such additions as will be made to the population within seven years.

It has long been a favorite boast that American agriculture could feed the world; but a critical examination of its further possible development brings us face to face with a state of affairs suspected only by the few, and shows plainly that long before the close of this century the increase in population and the inevitable exhaustion of the arable soils will necessitate one of two things, namely, the adoption, on the part of the great mass of the people, of a less liberal standard of living or the importation of food. Probably the ability to support a greater population will come from a resort, in some measure, to the first of these alternatives.

The average American, ambitious and somewhat extravagant in his mode of living, will be reluctant to reduce the standard, and only the enhanced cost of indispensibles will impel him thereto.

By the adoption of a more economical way of living, and by the increased production which may follow improved culture, the per capita requirements can probably be reduced from 3.16 acres to 3 acres, when the land now in cultivation and that which can be brought into cultivation will sustain a population of 82,000,000—a number that will probably be reached soon after the close of the century—while two, three or four decades will doubtless be required to bring the remnants of the arable areas into production.

This seems the more probable in view of the fact that the average rate of increase in cultivated acres during the last five years has been but 1.6 per cent. per annum, as against 8.4 per cent. ten years earlier, and that it must grow less and less continuously, by reason of the constant shrinkage in the quantity of arable lands subject to draft; hence it would be a most liberal estimate to place such increase, during the remainder of the century, at an average of three-fourths of one per cent. per annum, which would, in 1900, make the cultivated area devoted to staple crops some 226,000,000 acres, or sufficient, at 3.16 acres per capita, for a population of 71,500,000 (and at 3 acres per capita, for a population of 75,300,000), with the possibility of adding from 15 000,000 to 20,000,000 acres more in the earlier decades of the twentieth century. This, however, is an extremely liberal estimate, while a reasonably cautious one would put the rate of increase in cultivated area, during the remainder of the century, at one-third the rate obtaining since 1884, or an average of one-half of one per cent. per annum. That would in ten years augment the cultivated area by 10,500,000 acres making an aggregate of some 221,500,000 acres, or sufficient, at 3.16 acres per capita, to meet the requirements of 70,000,000 people. and at 3 acres per capita, of 74,000,000, which is probably as large a population as our fields can provide for during this century.

In view of the progressively rapid reduction in the rate of increase, and the constantly diminishing quantity of unoccupied arable land to draw from, an addition of 10,500,000 acres of cultivated land seems to be quite as much as can be expected in this decade. During the remainder of this century, the annual increase in consumption will necessitate average yearly additions of 16,000,000 acres to farm areas, of which nearly one-third must be land actually producing staple crops. With but 100,000,000 arable acres to draw from, of which a considerable part is already included in farms, there would appear to be little difficulty in determining the maximum time that will elapse before the exhaustion of the material from which new farms can be carved in numbers sufficient to meet the requirements of the increasing population, and after which consumption must, as in Europe, be met from the products of a given and practically unexpanding area supplemented by an importation of food.

SOME IMPENDING CHANGES.

When we reflect that the prime factor in the unexampled prosperity of the United States, and our comparative freedom from many of the social and economic problems long confronting Europe, has been the existence of an almost unlimited area of fertile land to which the unemployed could freely resort; that, practically, such lands are now fully occupied, and that such occupancy has occasioned a sudden halt in the westward movement of population at the line found to be the extreme western limit of profitable agriculture, it may be well to inquire what changes are likely to result from the exhaustion of the tillable portion of the public domain.

That settlement and cultivation, more or less complete, have overrun and occupied all the tillable lands, with the exception of small tracts held for higher prices, is shown by the reversal of the current of population which, for three or four years has been moving eastward from the great plains lying at the base of the Rocky Mountains, after the units constituting this army of returning settlers have each spent years in futile efforts to extort the means of subsistence from a soil lacking only moisture to render it fruitful.

Year following year the crops have failed, and the settlers upon these arid wastes, after exhausting their limited means, have, in a majority of cases, been forced to abandon their lands and improvements, representing a life's savings Such experiences have probably been necessary in order to demonstrate the exhaustion of the arable lands.

It is the more or less complete elimination of this factor in the prosperity of the country which is the presage of rapid and far-reaching changes in the social, economic, industrial and political relations of the people. Heretofore, when the invention of a labor-saving device threw numbers of men out of employment, a portion, especially of the more thrifty, resorted to the public domain, from which they proceeded to carve a farm, or bought the farms of others contemplating removal to the public domain, in or cases, found employment in one of the many channels constantly being opened for labor in the improvement of the new States.

Weary of the city and its hopeless struggles, thousands were yearly resorting to the public domain while other thousands, unable speedily to encompass their desires in this direction, still hope that industry and economy will yet enable them to secure a home in the limitless West, and will not realize that there are no more free lands worth owning until they have made such costly and fruitless experiments as have the people now marching eastward from the arid plains.

To the capitalist, the settlement and development of the new States has presented an inviting field, and here have been laid the foundations of many of the great fortunes which excite the wonder and astonishment of Europeans. In this undeveloped region the capitalist and speculator have found a new field for exploitation, possessing, in latent form, wonderful mineral, woodland and agricultural resources and fast filling with a restless race of workers and consumers, and a vast territory without railways, factories or mines, the construction or development of which promised and furnished profitable employment to an immense capital.

Here the railway projector and builder found ample opportunities for fame and fortune; the mine operator, rich mines of coal, and all the useful and precious metals; the money-lender, men in almost countless numbers, ready to pay high rates for the means enabling them to buy this piece of property or improve that, to erect mills and factories, open and equip farms, build cities and bridge streams, until the West became, for the eastern owner of capital, a veritable Pactolian stream, and western farm mortgages were esteemed the best of gilt edged securities.

Now, however, all this is about to change—is changing. The investor in railway securities cannot much longer invest all his surplus income in the bonds and shares of of new lines, as little new mileage will be either needed or built outside of the Southern and Pacific States; towns will expand, but few new ones will be built; new factories and forges will rise, and new mines be opened, but local capital will largely be employed in such enterprises and to those interested in railway securities the change means a lessened rate of income, fewer opportunities for profitable investment in new lines, the old lines largely double tracked, new and more commodious equipment, better methods of administration, less manipulation for the exclusive benefit of those active in the management and greater efforts to serve the public, and thereby evade the restraining arm of the law.

For the owners of buildings it means lower rentals, continuous improvements in order to keep the property up to an advancing standard and a rate of income shrinking as does the rate of interest.

The implication for the manufacturer is a broader and more exacting home market —as the farmer, receiving for his products from 50 to 100 per cent. more than now, will become a vastly more liberal and discriminating buyer—for his wares, which must be sold at a lower price, offset by lower interest charges and relatively cheaper raw materials of foreign origin, and, if the manufacturer is to furnish employment to all who seek to enter his service, it indicates a search for distant markets and a sharp competition with Europe for the trade of other continents. To the possessor of loanable funds it means a constant shifting of investments to inclined planes where the returns will, by reason of a constantly increasing competition from an augmenting supply of capital seeking investment, continuously diminish, and a probable restriction of choice in investments, the proportion of borrowers being likely to lessen.

That the West is, even now, in large part emancipated from monetary dependence upon the East, was made manifest during the flurries of last Autumn in the money markets of New York, Boston and Philadelphia, when the western exchanges pursued the even tenor of their way, with but little oscillation in rates, and with loans about as readily procurable as usual.

Producing so largely of the useful and precious metals, and with an advance of 50 to 100 per cent. in the price of the agricultural staples so indispensable to human life, and which are so largely grown in the Mississippi valley, the West will soon receive immense accessions of capital, and—as one of the results of the exhaustion of the arable portion of the public domain—is like to become the creditor section at a very early day. Moreover' the products of manufacture consumed by the western people will, with no more farms to open by the increasing population, be from year to year more and more the out-turn of western establishments.

The farmer, while engaged in opening and equipping his farm, with prices often on a parity with or below the cost of production, has been forced to become a borrower, and after paying interest and taxes, has had barely the necessities of life. Now, however, with the relative number of his competitors yearly lessening, both at home and abroad, better prices obtaining, with an assurance—arising from an increase in the population out of proportion to any possible increase in the area under cultivation—that well within ten years such prices will double, there is every reason to believe that he will cease to be a debtor.

Without the possibility of the further material expansion of the cultivated area, will come a restriction of new enterprises, fewer chances to make great fortunes, and a steadier and more settled social life for the comfortable classes; and although for a time the young man may not find the difficulties attending a start in life seriously increased, yet with the next generation the way will, as a rule, be open only to him who has wealth or social influence at his command. In other words, we shall place the same value upon such influences, and find the opportunities for a career to depend on much the same conditions as now obtain in Western Europe.

For the artisan and laborer the impending change points, in the near-by years, to a brisker demand for his services, as the farmer becomes a more liberal buyer and builder.

To the farmer the exhaustion of the arable lands will bring changes most desirable. Not competing with the whole world for glutted foreign markets, the demand for his products will be steadier, and being quite sufficient to absorb all his commodities and divest the option dealer of much of his pernicious power over prices, which will for years advance steadily, as demand will soon and progressively outrun production, thus enabling him to discharge his debts; to build better houses, barns and granaries; provide more and better furniture and clothing, and, where it exists, to gratify a love for books and works of art, and to surround his family with the comforts and many of the elegancies of life now enjoyed by other classes, but which a meagre income has placed beyond his reach.

It means that the coming generation of farmers will labor less, read and think more and to better purpose, and many of the sons and daughters be educated at the higher seats of learning, and thus be enabled to take a creditable part in the world's work, and that all the brightest sons of the country side will not desert the farm, as it will promise something beyond a life of unrequited toil.

By the invention of labor-saving devices, and their use on farms sufficiently large to warrant the purchase of a full line of improved implements, one man is now able to produce three times as much as forty years ago, and nearly twice as much as twenty years since, and although there seems little reason to expect in future as great reduction in the labor involved in the production of staple crops, it is altogether probable that such further mechanical improvements will be made as will enable a force equal to that now employed on the farms to cultivate all the land which will be in use in 1910; hence there will be a constant movement of population from farm to town, the rural population augmenting only in so far as that great numbers of working proprietors will, at no remote day, be able to and will employ laborers to till their fields. With a birth-rate quite as great as that obtaining with the urban population the rural districts will contribute not less than 75 per cent. of their increase from births—6,000,000 before 1910—to the town population, necessitating a constant widening of the markets for American manufactures.

After the middle of the tenth decade we need not be solicitous about a market for farm products, and treaties providing for the free entry of foreign commodities in consideration of the free entry into other countries of the products of American farms will need revision in the interest of American manufactures not later than 1895, as we shall then have only such agricultural staples as cotton, tobacco and, possibly, meats for export.

Careful computations have been made of the probable increase of population and the area likely to be in cultivation at the end of each quinquennial period up to and including 1910, adopting lower rates of increase, in population, especially after 1895—than are generally current, it being assumed that the number of immigrants will gradually diminish from natural causes and restrictive legislation, and that as the difficulties attending the maintenance of a family increase marriage will occur later in life and smaller families result. On the other hand, in estimating the increase in the area likely to be under cultivation, the rates adopted are higher than the great scarcity of tillable land and the rates of increase—progressively lessening—obtaining in recent periods warrant, it being deemed best to make this estimate so liberal that if there be error it shall take the form of a larger area than is likely to be in cultivation.*

Estimates of the area required for domestic consumption are based upon the mean of population and the area under such crop during the last ten years, as reported by the Department of Agriculture, after deducting from such area the proportion employed in growing that part of the crop exported and the acreage per capita quota stated is that found necessary to produce only so much of the staple farm products as is required for home consumption except in the matter of cotton and tobacco, which it is assumed we shall continue to export long after we find it necessary to import food, as the cotton lands are, as a rule, but poor wheat lands, and the commercial world will long be unable to dispense with American cotton, the price of which will advance as do the prices for other agricultural staples; hence southern fields will continue to bring the most satisfactory returns while devoted to cotton growing.

Eliminating the doubtful factors from the computations, it is found that the population will, in 1895, probably reach 70,000,000, each unit requiring 3.16 cultivated acres to provide the staple food products, provender and materials for manufacture consumed at home, and permit the exportation of the same proportion of cotton and tobacco as now, the aggregate requirements being 221,200,000 acres as against the 220,000,000 which it is estimated will then be in cultivation, the deficit amounting to 1,200,000 acres and indicating the importation of food.

At the close of the century population will probably have increased to 77,000,000, and, consumption continuing at the same rate per capita as now, we shall need the product of 243,000 000 acres; and with but 226,000,000 in cultivation, the necessity for the importation of food will long have been imperative.

Ten years later it is estimated that population will have increased to 90,000,000, the area in cultivation to 234 000 000 acres and the requirements to 284,000,000—the dficit reaching 50,000,000 acres, or 18 per cent., and necessitating the importation of nearly one-fifth the food and provender consumed, *or a proportionate lowering of the standard of living.*

During the twenty years which will be required to add 27,000,000 to our population that of Europe will probably increase 70,000,000, that of the La Plata countries 4,000,000, and that of Canada, Australia, New Zealand, South Africa and other European colonies fully 10,000,000; so that by 1910 the wheat-eating populations of European blood will have increased at least 100,000,000, requiring an addition to the world's supply of rye and wheat of no less than 700,000,000 bushels, of which about 450,000,000 bushels should be wheat.

It is barely possible that in twenty years the European product may increase 30,-000,000 bushels that of North America 50,000,000, that of South America 30,000,000, that of Australasia 20,000,000, and that of India, Persia, etc., 20,000,000, making a possible total increase in product of 150,000,000 bushels as against an increase in requirements three and a half times as great. Any increase whatever, either in the United States, Europe or India, is more than doubtful, as the European area employed in growing wheat and rye has shown no expansion during the last twenty years; the lands of India are fully occupied and the miserably nourished population ever pressing with increasing weight upon inadequate means of subsistence, and in the United States the wheat area is no greater now than in 1880. Moreover, the lands of Europe are so fully occupied as to preclude an increase in cereal production except in Russia and the Danubian countries, and any increase of the cereal area in Eastern Europe will be more than offset by the continued conversion of grain fields to the growth of other necessary products in Western Europe—products that will not bear transportation as well as grain.

*See "Exhibit 1", of the "Epitome of the Agricultural Situation" following page 24.

In the United States we must, in order to secure any permanent increase in the wheat area, unduly diminish the area in staples just as essential and even more difficult to import, although the importation of an adequate supply of wheat does not promise to be an easy task, as supplies—throughout the world—are certain to be so short as to ensure an eager scramble among the buying nations—including all Europe west and south of Hungary—and still leave an unsatisfactory deficit.

Such will be some of the results following the exhaustion of the arable portion of the public domain of the United States, accompanied by much higher prices for the agricultural products of temperate climates, a great world-wide and enduring advance in the value of lands in the temperate zones susceptible of profitable cultivation, and the unexampled prosperity of the landlord and cultivating proprietor.

Of late years the returns of the American farmer and the European cultivator have been but little more than sufficient to afford a meagre subsistence; but granting the approximate correctness of the estimates made, it is inevitable that the relations of supply and demand should, in the immediate future, undergo such radical changes as to cause prices to advance steadily and rapidly to fifty, one hundred and possibly two hundred per cent. above the level now obtaining; and such advance, however great it may prove to be, will be so much added to the landlord's rent and the cultivator's profit. As present prices cover the cost of production, and such cost is far more likely to diminish than augment, the advance in the price of farm products will accurately measure the advance in the value of land. Hence if the returns now cover the cost of production with wheat selling at 90 cents per bushel and the average yield twelve bushels per acre, when it shall sell for $1.80 per bushel the returns will have increased by $10.80 per acre, and assuming that only one-half the farm will be so employed as to make such net returns and that money—twenty years hence—will, on real estate security, loan at three and one-half per cent. we find the value of such lands to be quite $150 per acre and equaling the value reached by the lands of France prior to the great shrinkage in value occasioned by the low prices for farm products prevailing in recent years. On this basis, should the farms and gardens of the United States, in 1910, cover an area of 750,000,000 acres (including pasture, woodland and waste), as is altogether probable, their value, exclusive of the live stock and implements, will reach the enormous sum of $112,500,000,000 and their owners will, with the owners of other real estate, form a great landed interest which, in its magnitude, will long exceed and overshadow all others and with an influence far more pronounced than now, although their numbers will be proportionate less, make for steadiness, peace and order in social industrial and political life.

The converse of this class is likely to be found in the ranks of labor increasing more rapidly than other of the social elements by reason of the continuance, for some years, of immigration, of an inability to make further drafts from the ranks of labor to the public lands, and the advance of land values precluding the purchase, by this class, of as many improved farms as heretofore, and by large accessions from a rural population that, unable to open new farms, increases four or five times as fast as rural employments, and which must in the absence of railway construction and forests to be felled, of necessity swell prodigiously the increasing myriads seeking employment in mine, factory and forge.

Adding to an industrial population, now nearly sufficient to supply all the wares imported, three-fourths the increase of the rural districts, we shall, before 1910, in this manner alone, swell the urban population by more than 6,000,000; or, in other words, of a total increase of 27,000,000 during the next twenty years, fully 25,000,000 will be found, with other 40,000,000, in mine, village, town and city.

To employ these people our rulers must, in the absence of the safety-valve heretofore existing in the public domain, find means of opening distant markets which shall absorb the labor of this vast force multiplied by the progressive improvement and employment of machinery which each year will bring.

Europe has long confronted a somewhat similar state of affairs, with the very important difference, however, that America has been able to furnish sufficient grain and meat to keep the price of food at a much lower level than seems longer possible.

In 1910, with an urban population of 65,000,000, it may be necessary, in order to employ such an enormous force, to adopt such a fiscal policy as will ensure the free entry of all materials entering into manufactures which we are unable to produce, and to so levy imposts as in no measure to lessen our ability to compete with Europe for the trade of the world, and thus postpone, to the latest possible day, that social condition necessitating emigration to South America, Australia or Africa.

THE FARMER IN THE COMING CHANGE.

Twenty years since, wherever the cultivator owned the land he occupied he was exceptionally prosperous and so continued to be until about the middle of the eighth decade, when the opening of so many new farms in the Missouri valley and the development of Indian wheat exportation so changed the relations of supply and demand for food products that prices fell greatly and the farmer's revenue, from a given area, was much lessened; yet it is more than questionable if this lowering of the price of food has resulted beneficially to the industrial classes, although it has enabled them to buy their food for less money, yet probably such food has, because of the disastrous change in the farmer's condition, actually cost them more labor than it would had prices remained at the level obtaining during the first half of the eighth decade, when the price (in gold) of English grown wheat, in the markets of Great Britain, was 85 per cent. greater than the price obtaining in the same markets in the year 1890, as the changed conditions surrounding the employment of the capital and labor of the farmer have, in a very large measure, destroyed the purchasing power of the most numerous class of the customers of the merchant, manufacturer, artisan and laborer.

The agricultural population of the United States number some 25,000,000 and is forty per cent. of the whole and when the purchasing power of such a great proportion of the people has been destroyed or greatly diminished it means lessened employment for others, lower wages as well as a lessened purchasing power on the part of all the industrial classes, more or less commercial stagnation, hard times, a descending scale of land and other values and increased indebtedness on the part of the producing classes, whose wares are selling at or below the cost of production. This has long been the case with a very considerable part, if not the whole, of the agricultural class and has resulted in less power to purchase the products of the labor of others, who, in turn, have thereby had their purchasing power diminished so that the whole economic fabric has been subjected to unprofitable conditions which have affected all classes alike, if in varying degrees.

In the case of the American, as well as all other farmers, the reduction in his returns has been abnormally great, as the prices of farm products—as measured by the price of wheat—were 85 per cent. greater during the first half of the eighth decade than those obtaining during the year just closed, and this change in price very accurately measures the change in his purchasing power and the result is that he wears last year's coat, buys little or no hardware, puts up few or no new buildings, makes the old buggy last another year, the daughter has to do without the promised musical instrument, the son cannot secure the expected education and the makers of hardware, coats, books, pictures, organs, pianos, furniture and carriages and teachers, transporters, merchants, jewelers, professional men and artisans are but half employed, and find it more difficult to buy flour made from seventy-five cent wheat than they would if wheat had never sold below $1.50 per bushel.

This state of affairs has, however, under the conditions which have existed in this country, probably been inevitable, and while many such auxiliary causes as the unreasonable exactions of the transportation companies and the far-reaching and baleful practices of the Board of Trade gambler in farm products have been largely contributory, the primary and potent cause lies deep down in that desire of the race to own a home and to sit, each man, under his own vine and fig tree which has found such wide scope for its realization on the public domain, where all were welcome to a farm without money or price; and this, in the absence of a retarding forest growth, resulted in an increase of 112 per cent. in the cultivated area of the United States during the fourteen years ending with 1885, while population increased but 44 per cent.

During the last half decade, however, a radical and far-reaching change has obtained —obtained because the raw material from which farms are made has been practically exhausted—and while population continues to increase in nearly as great a ratio as prior to 1885, or 12.5 per cent., the cultivated area increased but seven per cent., and the rate of the acreage increase is yearly and progressively lessening, one consequence being that the quantity of land employed in the production of food for exportation has diminished from 21,000,000 acres in 1885 to 10,000,000 acres in 1891, and continuing to diminish at the same rate will, by 1895, have wholly been absorbed by the requirements of our added population.

The following table shows the rapidity of agricultural development and the progressively decreasing rate at which additions are being made to the cultivated area and indicates the early coming of that time when the American, and especially western, farmer will be the most prosperous member of the community:

EXHIBIT SHOWING INCREASE OF CULTIVATED AREA IN THE UNITED STATES AND THE RATES PER CENT. OF INCREASE.

	1871	1875	1880	1885	1890
Cultivated Area in Staple Crops, Acres..............	93,000,000	123,000,000	165 000,000	197 000,000	211,000,000
Increase of Cultivated Area in Each Period Acres.....'	....	30,000,000	42,000,000	32,000,000	14,000,000
Rate per cent. of Increase in Each Period:.............	....	32.2	34.1	19.4	7.1
Increase of Cultivated Area Each Year during Each Period, Acres.... ....'	....	7,500,000	8,240,000	6,400,000	2,800.000
Yearly Rate per cent. of Increase during Each Per'd	....	8.1	6.8	3.9	1.4

The preceding table shows that during the fourteen year period ending with 1885 the increase in cultivated acres was not less than 112 per cent. as against an increase in population of 44 per cent. This phenomenal increase was not only sufficient to meet the requirements of the great additions made to our own population, but also *quite sufficient to meet the additions made to the European populations and still leave a surplus to be stored as reserves*, which have been drawn upon in later years when current production has been less than current needs. Now, however, our additions to the area under cultivation are less than equal to half our added needs

Concurrently with the addition of so many new farms in the United States the Indian government abrogated the export duty upon wheat and Indian exports that aggregated but 464,000 bushels in 1871 rose, in 1887, to 41,500,000 bushels without, however, any increase of the Indian wheat area; indeed the area sown to wheat at the close of the ninth decade was a million acres less than in 1870, the augmented exports being very largely due to the increasing and inconceivable poverty of the Indian cultivator who has been obliged to sell an ever increasing proportion of his crop—as the price fell—to pay the constantly augmenting land (rent) tax, although a population increasing three times as fast as the cultivated acreage actually required this food for home consumption.

The result of such a disproportionate increase of population and cultivated acreage in the United States and the compulsory exportation of wheat by the starving Indian ryots is seen in the fact that whereas, during the five years ending with 1875 the average price (in gold) of English grown wheat in the markets of Great Britain was $1.64 per bushel, it was but 95 cents during the five years ending with 1890. In other words wheat —which is the key to the agricultural situation—during this fifteen years shrank in selling price, in consequence of the opening of so many American farms and the development of Indian exports, no less than 69 cents per bushel, and the price of all other primary staple food products have shrunken in like proportion. Is it any wonder that times are hard and stagnation everywhere when the fountain has been dried at its source?

The price of wheat having been 73 per cent. greater for the five years ending in 1875 than during the last five years, it follows that the purchasing power of the farmer has been lessened in nearly like measure, although there has been some little reduction in the cost of production. Add again this proportion to the purchasing power of the immense agricultural class of the United States and every artisan, laborer, miner, manufacturer, transporter, builder and professional man will be fully employed, wages good and the whole industrial life be quickened in an astonishing manner. It is almost impossible to conceive that such a change is impending after the experiences of recent years, when the farmer has seen. notwithstanding all his industry and privation, the debt, with its annual interest charges, yearly increasing. That such a change is impending and is susceptible of proof, as data exists, and but requires the labor and patience necessary to its gathering and tabulation, to show that there is a deficient acreage as well as a most direct relationship between population, acreage in staple food products, prices for such products and the prosperity of the cultivator, as well as the prosperity of all other classes, as there can be no doubt that all the industrial forces are just as dependent upon and just as intimately connected with, the property of the basic industry as in that remote past when the founder of the second Persian monarchy said: "There can be no power without an army; no army without money, and no money without a prosperous agriculture." In the view of this most successful statesman the farmer was the ultimate source of all wealth, as well as power, and to see that such is still the case we have only to watch the stock markets and observe how values rise and fall as the crops are full or meagre.

Many things have changed since the days of Artaxerxes, and industrial processes differ wonderfully, but the great underlying principles have not changed, and when the basic industry is in an unprosperous condition there will be but little money moving, and that little moving slowly through the arteries of industrial and commercial life, while the body politic will be in just the state we have seen during the period when the acreage devoted to the production of food increased more rapidly than the consuming population. Now, however, the condition of the farmer is changing for the better more rapidly than his affairs changed for the worse during the eighth and ninth decades.

Wheat production may be said to be the controlling factor in acreage distribution, as well in production, as the product is at all times and everywhere saleable at some price and it is the one product that the farmers of the temperate zone rely most upon to furnish the needed money. This is no less true of Russia than of Australasia; no less true of the United States than of India, and the result is that of the area now employed, in America, in producing food for exportation about eighty per cent thereof is devoted to the production of wheat.

During the eighth decade the wheat acreage of the world increased (in round numbers) 24,000,000 acres, or 15.6 per cent., and treating the compulsory exports of India as being equivalent to an addition of acreage, the additions to the supplies of the bread-eating populations of European blood was, during that decade, equal to the product of 27,000,000 acres, and the ascertained average yield per acre would give a yearly out-turn of 320,000,000 bushels; which, at 4.75 bushels per capita, was equal to the requirements of 67,000,000 people, while the bread-eating populations increased 41,000,000, so that had rye kept pace with the increase in the rye consuming part of the bread-eating world there would have been, at the end of the eighth decade, a surplus wheat acreage equal to the requirements of 26,000 000 people.

Assuming that the wheat acreage twenty years since—when prices were 73 per cent. greater than in 1890—was sufficient to meet the requirements of the then existing population we find the acreage, at the beginning of the ninth decade (treating the recently developed Indian exports as an increase of available acreage equal to the production of a like number of bushels), was some 9,500,000 acres in excess of requirements, and

being
added
pply,
out of
blood
serves
urplus
urplus

ld the
n, and
, adds
dly be
have

urplus
nuance
a great
austed.
and as
itional
and for
ion in-
50,000,-
e must
lly add
n years

s have
porting
only in
staples
otatoes,

an one-
on the
abroad,
. of the
sh more

domain
ation of
export
00,000,-
er food
ices, as
nd the
on con-
ance of
ill not
sixteen
ive his
es; his
ney he
rced to
r, they
hereas

AN EPITOME

OF THE AGRICULTURAL SITUATION, AND AN ESTIMATE OF AMERICAN PRODUCTION AND REQUIREMENTS FOR FOUR QUINQUENNIAL PERIODS.

during that decade there was added to such wheat producing area 4,164,000 acres (being but 2.3 per cent.) or an area equal to the requirements of 10,000,000 people which, added to the 26,000,000 which the surplus acreage, at the beginning of the decade, would supply, and we have, at the end of the ninth decade, a supply sufficient for but 36,000,000 out of the 56,000,000 that have been added to the bread-eating populations of European blood since 1880 the residue having, up to this time, been supplied by the enormous reserves that accumulated in mill, warehouse and farm granary during the existence of a surplus acreage, such reserves being now quite exhausted.

From the best data obtainable it would appear that with an average yield the world's crop of wheat is now 100,000,000 bushels less than the yearly consumption, and that each passing year, by reason of the increase in the bread-eating population, adds from twenty to twenty-five millions to this yearly deficit, so that by 1895 it can hardly be less than 200,000,000 bushels if the per capita requirements remain as large as they have been.

Up to the present time the reserves accumulated during the existence of a surplus acreage have sufficed to meet this deficit—such deficit in the five years of its continuance and growth having probably aggregated 300,000,000 bushels less the excess of the great crop of 1887-8—but there is abundant evidence that these reserves are everywhere exhausted.

The people of Europe yearly consume about three bushels of rye per capita, and as no additions have been made to the world's rye fields since 1870 there is an additional draft of something like 17,000,000 bushels with each recurring year to meet a demand for wheat created by the failure of the rye fields to expand as the rye-eating population increases, and this has consumed much of the world's surplus of wheat—probably 150,000,-000 bushels since 1880—hence each year's addition to the supply of wheat and rye must hereafter be from 43,000,000 to 44,000,000 bushels. In other words, we must annually add to our wheat and rye fields nearly 4,000 000 acres, while the additions of the last ten years have been but 400,000 acres per annum.

All additions to the area devoted to the two principal bread-making grains have ceased in Europe as a whole; have ceased in the United States, and among the exporting countries such area is increasing only in Canada, Australia and Argentina, and only in Argentina does it keep pace with domestic requirements. The other primary food staples show a somewhat greater relative increase, but, taking all kinds of grain and potatoes, they are increasing less than one-half as fast as the consuming population.

Of recent years the cultivated acreage of the United States increasing less than one-half as fast as the domestic requirements, we are yearly making great inroads upon the acreage heretofore employed in producing the grain and animal products sent abroad, and while we now export—exclusive of cotton—something less than six per cent. of the products of our farms, this percentage must, from increasing home needs, diminish more than one-fifth per year.

Owing to our inability to make further considerable drafts upon a public domain that has been practically exhausted of its tillable portion and the rapid augmentation of domestic population and requirements, it appears probable that we shall cease to export food at the end of five years, and as the world will then be annually short some 200,000,-000 bushels of wheat and a still greater quantity of rye, to say nothing of other food staples, high prices must then obtain, but we need not wait five years for high prices, as the deficient acreage now obtaining ensures such prices from this year forward, and the impossibility of making good this deficit in the world's food areas, while population continues to increase at anything near present rates, assures the prolonged continuance of such prices and high prices for the products of the farm means that the farmer will not much longer be under the necessity of working on an average from fourteen to sixteen hours per day and that he will soon take his rightful place in the world and receive his share of the good things of life. He will build better houses, barns and granaries; his land will rapidly double and treble in value, and being able to secure what money he actually requires from the sale of only a portion of his produce, he will not be forced to sell when all others are doing likewise; hence, while prices will be so much better, they will also be far steadier and fluctuate only as affected by supply and demand, whereas

24

selling pri
velopment
primary st.
times are h
The
1875 than
has been le
the cost of
mense agri
facturer, tr
and the w
impossible
years, whe
debt, with
ing and is
necessary t
as a most d
for such pr
other class
upon and
that remot
no power
agriculture
source of a
to watch tl
meagre.
Man
differ won
basic indu
and that li
the body p
devoted to
Now, how
bis affairs
Whe
as well in
and it is tl
the needec
United St
America,
the produ
Dur
numbers)
as being e
eating po
27,000,000
of 320,000
67,000,000
kept pace
would ha
requirem
As
cent, gre
populatic
develope
of a like

during that decade there was added to such wheat producing area 4,164,000 acres (being but 2.3 per cent.) or an area equal to the requirements of 10,000.000 people which, added to the 26,000,000 which the surplus acreage, at the beginning of the decade, would supply, and we have, at the end of the ninth decade, a supply sufficient for but 36,000,000 out of the 56,000,000 that have been added to the bread-eating populations of European blood since 1880 the residue having, up to this time, been supplied by the enormous reserves that accumulated in mill, warehouse and farm granary during the existence of a surplus acreage, such reserves being now quite exhausted.

From the best data obtainable it would appear that with an average yield the world's crop of wheat is now 100,000,000 bushels less than the yearly consumption, and that each passing year, by reason of the increase in the bread-eating population, adds from twenty to twenty-five millions to this yearly deficit, so that by 1895 it can hardly be less than 200,000,000 bushels if the per capita requirements remain as large as they have been.

Up to the present time the reserves accumulated during the existence of a surplus acreage have sufficed to meet this deficit—such deficit in the five years of its continuance and growth having probably aggregated 300,000,000 bushels less the excess of the great crop of 1887-8—but there is abundant evidence that these reserves are everywhere exhausted.

The people of Europe yearly consume about three bushels of rye per capita, and as no additions have been made to the world's rye fields since 1870 there is an additional draft of something like 17,000,000 bushels with each recurring year to meet a demand for wheat created by the failure of the rye fields to expand as the rye-eating population increases, and this has consumed much of the world's surplus of wheat—probably 150,000,-000 bushels since 1880—hence each year's addition to the supply of wheat and rye must hereafter be from 43,000,000 to 44,000,000 bushels. In other words, we must annually add to our wheat and rye fields nearly 4,000 000 acres. while the additions of the last ten years have been but 400,000 acres per annum.

All additions to the area devoted to the two principal bread-making grains have ceased in Europe as a whole; have ceased in the United States, and among the exporting countries such area is increasing only in Canada, Australia and Argentina, and only in Argentina does it keep pace with domestic requirements. The other primary food staples show a somewhat greater relative increase, but, taking all kinds of grain and potatoes, they are increasing less than one-half as fast as the consuming population.

Of recent years the cultivated acreage of the United States increasing less than one-half as fast as the domestic requirements. we are yearly making great inroads upon the acreage heretofore employed in producing the grain and animal products sent abroad, and while we now export—exclusive of cotton—something less than six per cent. of the products of our farms, this percentage must, from increasing home needs, diminish more than one-fifth per year.

Owing to our inability to make further considerable drafts upon a public domain that has been practically exhausted of its tillable portion and the rapid augmentation of domestic population and requirements, it appears probable that we shall cease to export food at the end of five years, and as the world will then be annually short some 200,000,-000 bushels of wheat and a still greater quantity of rye, to say nothing of other food staples, high prices must then obtain, but we need not wait five years for high prices, as the deficient acreage now obtaining ensures such prices from this year forward, and the impossibility of making good this deficit in the world's food areas, while population continues to increase at anything near present rates, assures the prolonged continuance of such prices and high prices for the products of the farm means that the farmer will not much longer be under the necessity of working on an average from fourteen to sixteen hours per day and that he will soon take his rightful place in the world and receive his share of the good things of life. He will build better houses, barns and granaries; his land will rapidly double and treble in value, and being able to secure what money he actually requires from the sale of only a portion of his produce, he will not be forced to sell when all others are doing likewise; hence, while prices will be so much better, they will also be far steadier and fluctuate only as affected by supply and demand. whereas now they are affected by his necessities, which impel him to market his products just when every one else is doing so, the result being seasons of glutted markets and low prices, which once down are hard to elevate, while the overmarketing in the earlier part of the harvest year places a wonderful power in the hands of the gambler, who unhesitatingly uses it to further wreck prices. Once the farmer is in a position to hold his products, until they are required for immediate consumption, the market wrecker will be divested of much of his pernicious power over prices as then it will be the amount of real stuff offering—not the fictions as now—which will determine prices.

The coming of this advance in the returns of the farmer means a most profound change in all political, industrial and financial relations, as the farmer will cease to be a borrower and this will necessarily cause a lowering of interest rates and the West producing, as now, an immense surplus of food staples which the East must have, great sums will yearly move permanently from the East to the West in payment for high priced farm products and this will result in converting the west from the debtor to the creditor section.

Results so desirable to farmers, east as well as west, and to all interested, directly or indirectly, in western property or securities will come because the consuming element of the bread eating world has more than caught up with that enormous development of agricultural lands that to the thoughtless seemed to make good the boast that we could feed the world.

SOME SURPLUS PRODUCING STATES.

Only the twelve States named in the following tables produce a surplus of the great food staples, while such States as Ohio, Michigan and Washington produce a surplus of wheat alone. Their entire acreage in food and forage staples being found to be less than the normal per capita quota of 2.85 acres, they are, notwithstanding the fact that their lands are above the average of the whole country in fertility, not clearly surplus producing States, hence are not included with those that are, although it is questionable upon which side of the line they belong.

From the data to be found in the accompanying pages, and in the broad sheet following page 24, it is clear that hereafter such States, districts and individuals as produce the staple products largely in excess of domestic needs will enjoy an unexampled prosperity, as they will be able to command very high prices for their surplus—prices so much greater than the average cost of production as to leave a very large profit, hence the most fertile districts will be the most prosperous and the surplus food producing States of the Mississippi basin, large areas upon the Pacific slope and limited districts in the mountain regions being exceptionally productive, it follows that the prosperity which they will enjoy will be equally exceptional.

If the conditions as to climate and fertility are equally favorable it would appear that such States as produce—relatively to domestic requirements—the greatest surplus of food would enjoy the greatest prosperity; the accumulation of wealth be greatest, and the advance of land values, such as to soon place them upon a par with those of the best of the older districts.

That we may get a definite idea of the present relative importance—agriculturally—of the several States that produce, and are likely to continue to produce, a surplus of the staple food crops it is best to resort to a tabular exhibit showing the areas in corn, wheat, oats, other cereals and potatoes, separately, the several States being placed in the order indicated by the total area of each under such crops.

States.	Acres in Corn.	Acres in Wheat.	Acres in Oats.	Acres in Other Cer'ls	Acres in Potatoes.	Total Acr'ge in Food Staples.
Illinois............	8,022,000	1,853,000	3,372,000	308,000	146,000	13,701,000
Iowa	8,860,000	1,685,000	2,567,000	333,000	188,000	13,633,000
Kansas............	5,776,000	8,600,000	1,303,000	205,000	139,000	11,023,000
Missouri........	6,796,000	1,603,000	1,413,000	63,000	86,000	9,961,000
Indiana..........	3,668,000	2,494,000	1,017,000	65,000	79,000	7,323,000
Nebraska	4,097,000	1,418,000	1,053,000	276,000	84,000	6,923,000
Minnesota......	768,000	3,144,000	1,500,000	419,000	82,000	5,913,000
Wisconsin	1,102,000	1,073,000	1,497,000	770,000	138,000	4,580,000
Dakotas..........	885,000	4,210,000	1,183,000	280,000	58,000	6,616,000
California........	160 000	8,300,000	71,000	317,000	61,000	4,409,000
Oregon	8,000	887,000	222,000	41,000	20,000	1,178,000
Totals.....	40,142,000	25,267,000	15,198,000	3,577,000	1,081,000	85,265,000

In this exhibit it is seen that the States named produce 51 per cent of the acres of corn; 65 per cent. of the acres of wheat; 59 per cent. of the acres of oats; 57 per cent. of the acres of barley, rye and buckwheat, and 43 per cent. of the acres of potatoes.

While Illinois takes first rank, Iowa, is, even now, a close second and soon likely to take the lead in total area under food crops, as she now ranks first in the matter of surplus production, and as the highest degree of prosperity is likely to result from the greatest production in excess of domestic requirements, it is probable that Iowa will long retain first rank while the relative rank, in the race for wealth, of the surplus producing States would appear to be very clearly indicated in the following table, where each State holds the place earned by its power to produce food in excess of present domestic needs, and wherein is shown the population, the area under food and forage staples, the number of people eaoh can subsist from the acreage now devoted to such crops, the number that could be subsisted by the cultivated acreage in excess of the present population and the per capita acreage under cultivation:

States.	Population.	Acres in grain, hay and pota.	At .55 acres per capita cultivat. educes acres equal to subsistence of...	Number of people in excess of pres. ent population cultivated acres would subsist	Acres per capita in food and for. age staples ......
Iowa..............................	1,912,000	17,300,000	6,070,000	4.158,000	9.10
Kansas..........................	1,427,000	12,300,000	4,316,000	2,889,000	8.63
Illinois..........................	3,826,000	18,200,000	6,385,000	2,559,000	4.76
Nebraska.......................	1,059,000	8,300,000	2 912,000	1,853,000	7.84
Minnesota.....................	1,302,000	7,700,000	2,702,000	1,400,000	5.91
Missouri........................	2,679,000	11,600,000	4,070,000	1,391,000	4.33
Dakotas.........................	512,000	7,800,000	2,736,000	2,224,000	......*
Indiana	2,192,000	9,200,000	3,228,000	1,036,000	4.20
Wisconsin......................	1,687,000	6,600,000	2,316,000	629,000	3.91
California.......................	1,208,000	4,900,000	1,719,000	511,000	4.05
Oregon	314,000	1,656,000	518,000	267,000	5.28
Totals......................	18,118,000	105,556,000	36.972,000	18,917,000	5.83

This showing is remarkable and very significant, making manifest, as it does, that of the 191,000,000 acres employed in the Republic in the production of grain, hay and potatoes no less than 105,500,000—or 55 per cent.—are to be found in the twelve surplus producing States, and while they have a population of 18,000,000 they now produce sufficient of the primary food staples for the subsistence (even at the present high standard of living) of 87,000,000 people. This, however, but inadequately measures their relative productive power, as such is the fertility of their lands that, aside from the production of such a great proportion of the primary staples, they are pre-eminent for an ability to produce the secondary forms of food as they do the animals used for draft and pleasure, as is

*The reports of the Department of Agriculture not showing the Dakotas separately, it is impracticable to determine the per capita acreage satisfactorily.

clearly shown in the following table, stating the number of horses cattle and swine in the United States, and in each of these States, on the first of January, 1891, as set forth in the report of the Department of Agriculture for that month:

	Horses.	Cattle.	Swine.
UNITED STATES...	14,057,000	52,895,000	50,625,000
Illinois...	1.124 000	2,859,000	4,944,000
Iowa...	1,095 000	3,959 000	5,921 000
Kansas	748,000	2,679,000	3,144,000
Missouri..	806,000	2,632,000	4,586,000
Indiana..	648,000	1,762,000	2 561,000
Nebraska...	558,000	1,770,000	2,310,000
Minnesota...	391,000	1,183 000	538 000
Wisconsin..	433,000	1,540,000	1,110,000
Dakotas...	237,000	951,000	429 000
California...	361,000	840 000	518,000
Oregon...	181,000	827,000	230,000
Totals..	6,582,000	21,002 000	26,291,000
Per cent. of whole............	47 per cent.	40 per cent.	52 per cent.

While the States named have but 29 per cent. of the population of the United States they have 55 per cent. of the acreage in the great food and forage staples, and, having a soil much above the average in fertility, produce 63 per cent. of the grain, hay and potatoes of the nation; 47 per cent of the horses; 40 per cent. of the cattle, and 52 per cent. of the swine.

If hereafter farm products are to rule as high in price as is implied by the world's deficient acreage, the exhaustion of the available lands and the disproportionate rates at which cultivated acres and population are and have, for years, been increasing then the three preceding tables would indicate that such States will long enjoy an unexampled prosperity, and that such as have the greatest cultivated acreage per capita—as have, in the order named, Iowa, Kansas, Nebraska and the Dakotas—would seem to have every assurance, by reason of a surplus proportionately the greatest, of being the exceptionally prosperous parts of the food-producing West.

Given a bread-eating popuntion—the world's—increasing at the rate of 14 per cent. In ten years and an acreage in grain and potatoes increasing at the rate of 7 per cent., it is only a question of time when scarcity and high prices will result.

As the farmers of the West become prosperous and farm lands advance in value so will prosper all other western interests and western town property enhance in value.

AN OPEN LETTER.

To John Williams, Esq., St. Louis, Mo.

Dear Sir : Referring to your letter of July 12th, I beg leave to say that my reasons for believing that good lands anywhere in the United States will be worth $100 an acre within five years, are as follows :

No matter how much or how little land there may be under wheat, we must have a given quantity under each of the other staples, as is succinctly set forth in the following exhibit as is the manner of arriving at such quantities.

Exhibit showing the acreage required per capita to furnish staples consumed in the U. S. and cotton exported, as computed from (last) ten years acreage and production as set forth in the reports of the Department of Agriculture, first deducting the proportion of tobacco and grain—including the secondary form of animals and animal products—exported.

	Acres.
Wheat	0.48
Corn	1.19
Oats	0.39
Hay	0.64
Barley, Rye, Buckwheat, Potatoes and Tobacco,	0.15
Cotton	0.31
Total of	3.16

Just as soon as we lessen the quantity of hay or any other staple (needed for domestic consumption) below the current requirements, the price of that product will advance out of all proportion to the price of other staples, and land will at once revert to the growth of the high-priced product and there will be a lessened production of one or more of the other staples, the price of which will rise if the quantity produced is less than current needs.

There is an exact and ascertainable ratio between population and the production of each and all of the farm staples entering into general consumption, and my investigations have been directed to the determination of this relationship.

With a surplus of land in cultivation, the product of which must be marketed abroad, it has not been as easy to determine this matter as it will be when this surplus has been eliminated, as the elimination of this surplus will enable us to see the more clearly the inexorable character of the law of demand and supply, and when our people shall require all our products he who runs may read the proportions of such relationship. That we have not seen it before is probably due to the fact that we have had too much land in cultivation, and *could increase any one product at will without diminishing the domestic supply of any other.* This is, however, about to change—and by ' *about*" I mean within five years—and such desirable change as is coming will be greatly hastened if we can deprive the short-sellers, or the "Boards-of-Trade," of their baleful power over prices.

We cannot, as you suggest, take the pasture lands to grow wheat and other cereals, as the moment we reduce the number of cattle (other than milk cows) below 530 to 1,000 people, just that moment beef will become the most profitable product of the farm and great multitudes will rush into the cattle business, as they did in the earlier part of the ninth decade, when the immense amount of unoccupied lands, existing in the plain and mountain regions, enabled them to swamp the cattle business and bury its devotees under an avalanche of low-priced animals. Such conditions, however, can never again obtain as unoccupied areas do not exist permitting any such increase in the relative number of cattle. Indeed, from this day forward there is abundant reason to believe that the ratio of cattle to people will constantly lessen and the cattle business become very profitable to the farmer.

Nor can you take the dairy pastures and convert them into grain fields, as the moment you do, and reduce the number of milk cows to less than 230 to 1,000 people, that moment the price of milk, butter and cheese will mount skyward and grain fields will be converted into meadows and dairy farms.

For each 1,000 units added to the population we must add 230 milk cows and a given number of horses, and but for the surplus of beeves now existing we should have to add 500 to 530 cattle (other than milk cows) and for every cow, steer or horse added we must add from six to seven acres to our farms, and of this from two and a half to three acres must be in pasture.

Instead of converting pastures into grain fields we must add to such pastures in a definite ratio, and having now more wheat land than is required to meet the demands of our own people we shall take these surplus wheat fields and grow thereon the corn, hay, oats, rye, barley, buckwheat and potatoes required at home as well as the tobacco and cotton we consume and export, and when all the land that is now in cultivation, and that will, in the meantime, be brought into cultivation, is employed in producing the food, provender and materials of manufacture which our people require—as it will be not later than 1896—we must either cease to export cotton and grow grain upon the cotton lands, *lower the standard of living*, or import food.

Such is the relationship between population and the production of staples that there is but one crop we can reduce the area of, for more than one year, and that is wheat.

It is true that we now have about 2,000,000 acres more of corn land than is required by the existing population, but population will certainly overtake the corn fields not later than 1893, and in all probability in 1892, and then we must either reduce the per capita consumption of corn or convert wheat lands into corn fields.

When I say there is now 2,000,000 acres surplus corn acreage, *I mean that the product of this two million acres now goes abroad in the form of grain, meat and dairy products*, and that not later than 1893 or 1894 we shall consume at home every pound of such product made from an average crop of corn *unless* we shall then have converted a part of the wheat lands into corn fields, as the additions made yearly to our population necessitate an addition, annually, of 1,800,000 acres to the corn fields.

Existing, as there does, an exact relationship between population and all the staple products of the farm—such ratio varying only as varies the standard of living—when we can determine the proportions of this relationship we can estimate the acreage and product required with just as much certainty as a finance minister can estimate the amount of revenue from any impost.

Having ascertained that the average yield of wheat, for a period of ten years, is 12.1 bushels per acre, and that the annual consumption has been 5.73 bushels per capita, we are able to say that, with average yields, each unit of the population requires 0.48 of an acre in wheat, and knowing the population and the rate at which it is increasing, we can assume that there will be over 70,000,000 people inhabiting the United States in 1895 and that they will—with an average yield—require the product of nearly 34,000 000 acres in wheat, and, applying the same process to each of the other farm staples, we determine that they will require 83,300,000 acres in corn, 27,300,000 acres in oats, 44,800 000 acres in hay, 10,500,000 acres in barley, rye, buckwheat, potatoes and—including that exported—21,700,000 acres in cotton, making a total of over 221,000,000 acres.

If we can determine, approximately, the area which will then be in cultivation—and I hold we can—we can then say how much in excess or how much short of current domestic needs our products will be with average yields, and this is what I have attempted to do in Exhibit 1 of the "Epitome"* sent you, and this, with the world's (well ascertained) deficient wheat and rye acreage, and which it will be wholly impossible to make good and then have such acreage keep pace with the increase in population, cause me to believe that, not later than 1896, any acre of land in the United States that will, without more than the average cost for fertilization and cultivation, produce average crops of food, forage or fiber will sell readily for one hundred golden dollars.

In this connection permit me to say that I have but just returned from a journey through Illinois, Iowa and the other grain-growing States, and when in Iowa was assured by farmers, merchants and bankers that the selling price of Iowa farms had advanced fully 25 per cent. within a twelve month with the demand brisk at the advance, and I found similar conditions obtaining in Illinois and the other great food-producing States.

*See "Epitome of the Agricultural Situation" following page 24.

The one menace to the prosperity of the American farmer is the practice of short-selling (or option dealing) upon the "Boards of Trade."

In order to so discuss option dealing, or the short selling of farm products, that the reader may understand what is the writer's conception of the term, it will be best to illustrate by saying that on September 30th:

"A" contracts to sell and deliver and "B" to receive and pay for 10,000 bushels of the speculative grade of wheat at $1.00 per bushel, delivered at seller's option in December. There are also forms of option dealing which boards of trade do not recognize as regular, but wink at, such as "puts and calls," and a process obtains called "ringing out" whereby a vast majority of deals are daily settled by a kind of clearing house operation without any intention or semblance of delivery.

Under the contract supposed "A" has the "option" of delivering the amount of wheat named at such time during the month of December as he may elect, the term "option" having reference solely to the time when, during the month named, the seller may declare the contract matured, but not one contract in ten thousand is ever carried into effect by the delivery of property, it being a matter of common notoriety that in 9,999 out of every 10,000 such transactions "A" neither owns nor expects to own the grain he contracts to sell and deliver, nor does "B" expect to receive the wheat he has entered into a contract to receive and pay for, the tacit understanding being that should the price of wheat, at maturity of contract, have advanced to $1.05 per bushel, "A" shall, instead of delivering to "B" 10,000 bushels, pay him the difference between the then market price and the contract price, which being 5 cents per bushel, "A" pays "B" $500.00. On the other hand, should the price have declined 5 cents, "B" would settle the deal by paying "A" $500.00.

In all time contracts entered into upon Boards of Trade (and this term is used to designate all exchanges where such contracts are made), with very rare exceptions, neither seller nor buyer own or expect to own a single pound of the commodities in which they pretend to deal; nor do they contemplate the delivery or receipt of such commodities, but each hopes the price will turn in his favor and enable him to win. Thus the transaction bears the same relation to commerce as does a wager upon a horse race, the only difference being that in one case a definite sum is at stake, while in the other the wager is an indefinite one that the price of wheat in some future month will vary from a stated sum, the amount of the wager being measured by such variation, and the winning party is determined, not by supply and demand, but by as incalculable a contingency as the preponderance of the "bull" or "bear" element when the contract matures.

After the making of such a contract, "A" is short on December wheat and is designated as a "bear," and "B" is long on December wheat, and is classed as a "bull."

As nine-tenths of the time more option dealers are interested in depressing than in advancing prices, the weight and influence of the speculative body is almost continually exerted in depressing prices. First comes the constitutional bear, who, from long habit of thought or a pessimistic mental tendency, has come to believe prices are always too high; then the professional bear, who, *knowing it is easier to depress than advance prices,* sells below the current price property he does not own, and whose winnings depending upon lower prices, exerts all his ingenuity in exaggerating the extent of the supply and fabrication of such reports of failures, panics, stringent money markets and the great breadth of and favorable conditions surrounding the growing crops as will tend to cause the "longs" to become panic stricken and throw their holdings on the market and thus depress prices to a point that will enable him to win. Next comes the speculator, who, being convinced prices are too low and must advance greatly, intends to profit by the expected rise, but being "out of the market" and desiring to get in as cheaply as possible, becomes an active and unscrupulous bear, exerting himself to the utmost to depress prices that he may buy the more cheaply and increase his margin of winnings. Thus the efforts of nearly all the devotees at this singular commercial shrine work for lower prices, being effectually aided by a constant fear, on the part of holders of contracts, that prices will recede and entail loss.

The bears act upon the knowledge that men can be terrorized into selling, and any improbable tale of disaster will have an influence; hence, when they raid the market the air is thick with rumors of failures, panics and wide-spread commercial disaster, coupled with the offering in a single day of more grain than there is in the country, the result being that the bull becomes, in turn, nervous, timid and then panic stricken, and being unable to respond to a call for increased margins, throws his grain overboard, adding greatly to the swelling tide and helping to further depress the price. These immense offerings result in disastrous effects upon prices and the prosperity of the producer, the prices for whose products are fixed by these operations.

"A," among thousands of others, having contracted to deliver what he does not own and is unable to buy, except at a price greater than that at which he has agreed to sell, resorts to all conceivable devices, falsehoods and misrepresentations to break the market and so cheapen products, before the maturity of his contract, as to leave a difference in his favor, or that will enable him to buy a like amount of speculative grain at a price lower than that named in his contract with "B."

What with multitudes of bears, with contracts maturing and a contingent of bulls anxious to "get in on breaks," an immense majority of speculators are ever working for low prices and offering hundreds of millions of fiat products, and with each drop in price having a profit, multiply the offerings, such additional tenders further depressing prices, and thus without possessing a pound of the product offered these men are, by one round in the grain-pits, able to depreciate in value the entire grain products of the country, such depreciation sometimes representing a large part of the year's earnings of millions of farmers.

How different is the course of the legitimate dealer owning or having the means of producing the commodities offered for sale. All his efforts are directed towards securing good prices, steadiness in demand and freedom from rapid and wide oscillations in values. The seller who is an owner of property never depreciates it value, nor does he depress prices by offerings of impossible quantities which it would be impractible to deliver.

On the other hand, the market wrecker is such an exceptional product of civilization, and short selling such a singular commercial method that dealer and method are alike unique, being the only person and method ever engaged in systematically depreciating what the person proposes to sell, by such method; and such phases of option dealing and Board of Trade methods are not inaptly characterized in the following paragraph from the Chicago *Herald*:

"The trouble with the Board of Trade seems to be that instead of being, as it ought to be, a body of intelligent merchants devoted to the advancement of legitimate business and an intelligent study of questions affecting the control of the products of the West and their direction to the Chicago market, they seem to have reached the level of a body of mere speculative "scalpers," living off the farmer, producing nothing and in no sense contributing by their industry to the general good."

Nothing could be more destructive of the interest alike of producer and legitimate dealer than the practices now obtaining on the Boards of Trade where for each unit of any actual product sold and delivered hundreds of thousands of fictitious units are offered at prices sometimes one to fifteen per cent. below the price obtaining for actual product, owing doubtless to the fact that the mill has not been invented which will convert figments into merchantable flour. Such practices result in abnormal and excessive fluctuations in values—fluctuations so rapid as to bewilder those on the spot, as is shown by a recent Chicago market report in the statement that:

"The uncertainty with which the market moved yesterday may be illustrated by an incident. One trader having purchased 25,000 bushels December wheat at $1 02¼ stepped out of the pit. He had been out but a moment when he heard a great hubbub, rushed in under the impression that the market was dropping on him, frantically inquired the price, was told it was "seven-eighths," sold his wheat at that price, and was cursing his luck over a loss of "three-eighths" when he heard the remark that it was a quick "bulge" and learned it was $1.04⅛ instead of $1.01⅞ and that he had a profit of two and five-eighths instead of a loss."

Such conditions could not obtain were men dealing in products instead of fictions, as an immense capital would be involved instead of insignificant margins and callow youths could not sell millions on a capital of a few hundred dollars.

Such fluctuations inevitably destroy legitimate grain buying for the purpose of holding for profit, whereas a few years since men could be found at every village in the producing districts who stored grain for an advance. Now, however, the buyer is so thoroughly impressed with the danger arising from these fluctuations that he hastens to sell his grain as soon as bought, and when shipping takes the precaution to sell to arrive, using the wire to effect sales, afraid to trust the market for a single day.

So completely is the producer and distributor at the mercy of those selling mere figments that the packer daily buying a thousand hogs, the products from which require months to cure, is forced to seek protection against excessive fluctuation by selling for future delivery an amount of product equal to that from the hogs bought, and thus guard against a possible loss resulting from fluctuations which the exercise of no amount of sound judgment will enable the business man to measure, as none can measure the vagaries of a pit full of frantic speculators whose operations are as devoid of business deliberation as of commercial morality.

The following telegram but faintly describes a scene in the provision pit, a scene well worthy the pencil of a Hogarth:

"The provision pit on the Board of Trade, which has been almost deserted for several weeks, has been filled, since the opening of the Board this morning, with a frantic crowd of yelling betters. As soon as the Board opened it became rumored that there was a "corner" in pork in contemplation, and a wild scramble of shorts to cover followed."

There is not an article that has known the blighting touch of the market-wrecking short seller that it is not hazardous for the legitimate dealer to handle, and grain is made a veritable shuttle-cock of by a body of men the majority of whom are known by the suggestive title of "scalpers" and whose entire capital is barely sufficient to buy a Board of Trade membership, or "margin" a purchase or two of fiat grain, and yet the Chicago Board of Trade, in its memorial to Congress opposing the passage of the Butterworth bill, says:

"The passage of this bill and its enforcement as a law would produce a commercial convulsion amounting to a national calamity. It would be a vital attack upon the very foundation principles of modern business methods and usages. It would be hostile to the commercial genius and spirit of the age. It would destroy a vast system for the economical handling of the agricultural products of the nation; a system which is in entire harmony with the progress of our civilization and which is a part of that civilization. It would disastrously disturb transportation interests of every kind, and it would in many ways, directly and indirectly, react injuriously upon the farmer, and that by the passage and enforcement of the proposed law the farmer will be bereft of a market for his products."

Such assertions leave the onus of proof with the proponents, but a thorough examination of the memorial fails to disclose a single fact in support of such statements, while it admits the pernicious character of option dealing and favors its suppression when carried on in bucket shops, where methods identical with those obtaining upon the Boards of Trade are in vogue. Hence the layman naturally believes the bucket shop no worse than the Board of Trade, and the Board of Trade enmity to the bucket shop to be the outgrowth of rivalry in business. The bucket shop being the logical corollary of option dealing. When option sales cease on Boards of Trade the bucket shop will cease to exist.

Aside from its postulates the memorial is compounded in about equal parts of sophistications, pretended solicitude for the farmer and special pleadings for the continuance of a system which the judgment of the people condemn and the abolition of which would not cause even a ripple upon the stream of trade much less commercial convulsion.

When we reflect that only cotton, grain, hog products, coffee and petroleum are the subject of option sales, while thousands of other commodities are readily bought and sold without the factitious aid of the market wrecking option dealer and have thus far escaped the blighting effects of board of trade methods and that the natural relation of supply and demand determines the price for nearly all such articles, one cannot but hope that Congress will, by the enactment of an effective measure, relegate the staples subject to board of trade manipulation to such commercial methods as suffice for all other commodities.

Outside of New York, boards of trade furnish no information as to the extent of option sales, but they are prodigious and exceed the entire product so dealt in many thousand times, while the "*offerings*" which do not mature into even option sales, are hundreds of times as much as the option sales, *and it is these limitless offers,* as much as sales, which depress prices. *If sales were confined to actual commodities and delivery necessarily followed maturity of contract, offers would be limited by the amount available for delivery.* Now, however, it is not unusual for as much fiat wheat to be sold in a day as there is of actual grain received in a year. For instance: On the 14th of April, 1890, New York speculators sold 44,000,000 bushels of fiat wheat, probably more than twice as much as reached that city during the year. While the "*offerings*" in a single day, at either Chicago or New York, are said to often exceed 300,000,000 bushels, such offerings having the intended effect of depressing prices. Although there is no means of determining the volume of such offerings or sales, yet we can get some idea from a few days option sales of wheat and cotton at New York, as set forth in the following table:

SALES AT NEW YORK.

	WHEAT.		COTTON.	
DATE.	Sales of Actual Wheat Bushels.	Option Sales of Fictitous Wheat Bushels.	Sales of Actual Cotton.	Option Sales of Fictitious Cotton.
1890.	Bushels.	Bushels.	Bales.	Bales.
April 8	63,000	18,400,000		
April 9	54,000	2,000,000		
April 12	1,800	10,080,000		
April 14	6,000	44,000,000		
September 3	8,000	8,000,000	369	86,600
September 4	32,000	6,400,000		150 200
September 15	62,000	7,240,000	1,586	81,700
October 22	12,000	4,000 000	518	120,100
October 23	64,000	3,000,000	328	90,600
October 24	35,000	4,600,000	405	155,800
Total	337,800	125,720,000	3,206	684,000

This table shows that during the days named, that for each bushel of wheat sold New York market wreckers sold 372 bushels of fiat grain, and for each bale of cotton sold 213 fictions, and *that it would require but 36 days for them to sell options equaling in amount an average wheat crop and 66 days to sell all the cotton grown in a year.*

RECEIPTS AT CHICAGO.

FARM PRODUCTS.			FARM PRODUCTS.		
THE SUBJECT OF OPTION SALES.			WHICH ARE NOT SOLD AT OPTION.		
	Bbls , Bushels and Lbs.	Value.		Bbls., No. Lbs. and Tons.	Value.
Wheat	13,348,069	$ 12,094,000	Flour	6,133,608	$ 30,668,000
Corn	74,208,908	33,395,000	Cattle*	2,707,627	116,519,000
Oats	52,184,878	15,655,000	Swine	4,921,712	54,222,000
Rye	2,767,571	1,660,000	Sheep	1,575,014	6,000,000
Barley	12,387,526	7,432,000	Horses	55,333	5,000,000
Flax Seed	4,403 268	6,071,000	Butter	105,402,121	21,180,000
Grass Seed	1,500,000	4,500,000	Cheese	52,611,089	4,735,000
Barrel Pork	54,451	17,945,000	Hides	98,820,817	8,000,000
Bacon	146,728,592	11,760,000	Wool	30,517,316	6,500,000
Lard	70,885,797	6,100,000	Hay	325,000	3,500,000
Total values		$106,612,000			$256,324,000

*Including calves.

That farm products can be readily marketed without the aid of option sales is made manifest in the foregoing table compiled from the report of the Chicago Board of Trade, which table shows that of $363,000,000 worth of staple farm products shipped to and through Chicago in 1888, but 29.3 per cent. were articles subject to option sales, while 70.7 per cent. were sold without aids which the Boards of Trade would fain have us believe are necessary to the farmer's continued existence.

The market wreckers lay great stress upon the difficulty of selling grain by sample, stating such to be the alternative in case purely speculative contracts are prohibited, but sample sales would be no more common than now, as as all grain below grade is sold by sample, as is much of the grade grain sold for cash, and grain will continue to be inspected and sold by grade; still, if necessary, the $12,000,000 worth of wheat reaching Chicago could be sold by sample as readily as the $21,000,000 worth of butter, as could the $15,000,000 worth of oats as well as the $14,500,000 worth of hides and wool, each hide and fleece being subject to separate inspection, as is every package of butter, while grain is inspected and sampled by car loads.

To the $256,000,000 in value of farm products shown to be exempt from option sales should be added at least $50,000,000 worth of dressed beef and hogs, milk, poultry, eggs, fruit, vegetables and vast quantities of other products of the farm marketed at or through Chicago, justifying the assumption that of the farm products reaching the great market, fully three-fourths enter into consumption without assistance from this peculiar commercial method.

The report of the Chicago Board of Trade for 1888 shows that during the five years ending with 1888, there was grown 11,040,000,000 bushels of wheat and corn, of which 1,077,000,000, or 9.8 per cent. only, reached the eight interior Board of Trade markets and much of this was counted twice, as grain is shifted from one such market to another, and Chicago and other cities include in their receipts the produce in transit. The grain reaching the seaboard markets cannot be counted as it has been included once, if not twice, at interior points, *hence it follows that Boards of Trade aid to the extent of less than ten per cent. in marketing farm products*, and granting the substantial correctness of estimates by an eminent merchant—who yearly distributes millions of dollars worth of farm products to commerce—"that the effect of option sales is to reduce, by more than ten per cent., the value of all grain, cotton and swine grown, and that in the past ten years the farmers of the United States would have received $1,000,000,000 more for their products had not short selling become a prominent and profitable method of fixing values."

The farmer would be the gainer if every Board of Trade and the option dealing market wreckers were sunk at the bottom of the sea and 9.8 per cent. of his grain and cotton was permitted to rot in the field, thereby saving the cost of harvesting and marketing that percentage while the remainder would sell for more than would the whole if subjected to the baleful touch of the market wreckers; hence it cannot work a hardship to the producer to be bereft of the option dealer's market.

If 90.2 per cent. of the grain grown and 75 per cent. of all farm products reaching the large cities can be readily sold without being made foot-balls of by bands of speculators why not the small remainder?

If the 27,000,000 bushels of wheat which reached Chicago during the year in the form of flour could be readily and economically handled without being made the subject of option sales, why not the 13,000,000 bushels which reached the same market in its primary form?

If Chicago can, without the aid of option dealers, furnish buyers for $54,000,000 worth of pork in the form of swine, why should it be essential to the farmer's prosperity that the $26,000,000 worth in secondary form should be subject to the option dealer's manipulation?

It is readily seen why flour and swine escape the direct touch of the market wreckers. The moment wheat is converted into flour and marked with the miller's brand, it is severed from the mass of indistinguishable grain and assumes an individual character and the option dealer having the hardihood to sell 10,000 barrels of "Pillsbury's Best" short would find himself at the mercy of the miller owning such brand.

Yet the price of flour is determined by the option dealer's manipulation of the wheat market.

Although swine cannot be shipped to market, stored and advances procured,—as the market wreckers assure us is necessary in order to enable the farmer to market his products—and their inclination to run violently down a steep hill prevents the option dealer from including them in his short sales, the farmer m. nages to market his swine (and other animals) quite as readily and profitably as he does his grain. Unable to subject the hog to his methods, the option dealer makes ample amends when the animal has been converted into secondary product, but it is singular, that while he sells pork, lard and bacon short, such parts of the swine as canvassed ham, sausage, pig's feet, etc., must be disposed of by such methods as obtained in the commercial world prior to the evolution of the option dealer, and yet such dealer's pernicious arts affect the market for the animal most injuriously, as the price of the hog is directly related to that for the packing-house products' over which the option dealer holds a sway.

Aside from farm products, in primary and secondary form. the sales of merchandise in Chicago,—at wholesale—during 1888 amounted to $437,500,000, all of which was marketed without aid from the option dealer.

By reason of its being the largest market for farm products and the number. activity and supreme audacity of its speculators, Chicago has become the most potent factor in fixing the prices for such products, *and yet that city handles less than four per cent. of the wheat and corn grown,* its power in this direction being out of all proportion to the volume of products h indled, and is directly attributable ,to and in exact ratio to the enormous quantities of fictitious stuff constantly pressed upon the market, and it is the daily offering, selling and buying of these figments, in million on million of units, that enables a few men, possessed of capital and credit sufficient to "margin" millions of such fictitious commodities, to dominate the markets of the country and determine prices.

If the system which creates and perpetuates such con litions is an outgrowth of civilization, no less so are lotteries, dram shops, pool selling and anarchism, but a majority of citizens believe one and all are excrescences to which the knife should be applied without hesitation.

Because certain methods are the outgrowth of civilization it does not follow that they are benign, and there is abundent evidence that the baleful results of option dealing are incomparably greater than those attending the unrestricted sale of lottery tickets, as the lottery, aside from its corruption of public morals, affects only those who voluntarily become its votaries, while Board of Trade dealing in fictitious commodities is as much a game of chance as is the lottery, and not only debauches the morals of those who actively participate, but affects the prosperity of every cultivator, as well as that of every one having business relations with him.

From the planting of the seed until the crop is garnered and sold, the speculator pursues it with misrepresentations which are intended to and do lessen the selling price of farm products, but should the making of contracts for future delivery, other than by owners or producers of commodities, be prohibited as against public policy, the interest, prompting the propagation of false reports would disappear.

The following from a dealer in variiable products outlines the situation:

"I am a commission merchant, receiving from the West car-loads of grain to sell. For every bushel sold by actual shippers hundreds are sold "short" by speculators and it is a fact, that almost all the so called grain speculators in Chicago are short sellers and so far from trying to advance prices are constantly endeavoring to depress them. A few years since Chicago was called a producers' market, but now it it recognized as the great bear market of *the world* with a large majority of the dealers and a preponderence of the capital of the Board of Trade on the bear side."*

Is it not strange, that a city adjacent to the producing districts and the natural entrepot for the grain produced, should be decrying the value of what we in the West have to sell, and is it not anomalous that most of the articles in the press are bear articles, and lastly is there any other country, with a surplus to sell, that is constantly trying to depress the value of that surplus?

* "Commission Merchant" in Chicago Tribune, January 11

THE FARMER, THE INVESTOR AND THE RAILWAY.

Agriculture having been the first industry of settled life, we may assume that the farmer has pursued his calling since the dawn of civilization; yet, necessary as have been such labors, he has borne many burdens from which his brothers have been exempt, doubtless owing to the difficulty experienced in forming combinations with his fellows for concerted action, while those representing aggregates of capital, being comparatively few in numbers, easily effect such combinations. This is especially true of the present era, and of those controlling the great mass of capital represented by the railways of the country, nominally amounting to $9,369,000,000; and appearing to equal 60 per cent. while being not over 30 per cent. of the capital invested in farms, yet the influence exerted upon economic and other questions by railway owners and farmers is in an inverse ratio to their respective numbers and the magnitude of their investments.

One is a compact force, disciplined, alert, living in the midst of the greatest activities: the other exceedingly more numerous, undisciplined, leading isolated lives and with few incentives to quickening thought.

Those familiar with the history of the last sixty years will not question the great benefits resulting from the construction of railways, or grudge the men who have carried forward these great undertakings a rich reward.

By the aid of the railway the wilderness has been made productive, countless farms brought within reach of the great markets, mines opened, mills, factories and forges built, towns and cities brought into existence and populous States carried to a higher development than would have been possible in centuries without such aids. Such are but a part of the beneficent results flowing from the construction of the railway.

While the builders of the railway have been exploiting a continent and piling up the greatest fortunes ever known, the farmer has taken an unproductive wilderness and literally hewn his way through the great forests which clothed seaboard and central region to the open prairie, there developing the most productive of States, continued his toilsome march up the arid slopes, scaled the mountains and planted orchard, vineyard and farm by the shores of the Western Ocean.

His labors have enabled the nation to flood the markets with a plethora of bread, meat and fiber; to meet the enormous expenditure of a devastating war; to repair the losses and havoc of those bloody days, and then to turn the balance of trade in our favor.

Willingly has the farmer performed this labor, expecting to share in the prosperity of the country, yet not always content with his part of the rewards, and coming to believe that those controlling the carriage of his products were exacting as toll more than a just proportion thereof. He has seen the carrier yearly adding to his property, building new lines from the tolls collected on the old, increasing his wealth and power and leaving a constantly lessening proportion of the proceeds arising from the sale of farm products to the grower. As population has increased railway property has grown in relative value, as has the power of those controlling it, and this increase has been very largely made from revenues derived from tolls levied to pay interest and dividends on the water in the bonds and shares, hence made at the expense of railway users, a large part of whom are farmers.

All are fairly prosperous except such as are engaged in the basic industry of civilization, and the one cloud in the industrial horizon is the unsatisfactory condition of a large part of an agricultural population numbering some 25,000,000, and the railway is chargeable with so much of this as results from the exaction of unjust tolls, and this inquiry is instituted for the purpose of ascertaining if the complaints, as to the unreasonableness of such charges, are well grounded.

The highest tribunals hold that railways are public trusts, and can exercise the power to enter upon and take private property solely in their public character; and that the exercise of such exceptional power can be defended only upon the ground that the good of the public can best be subserved by a corporation under obligation to treat all justly in rendering services which each citizen cannot perform for himself; that the State could perform the functions delegated to railway corporations, which are trusts organized for the service of the public and charged with remuneration for the private capital employed; that the corporations thus endowed must provide all needed facilities for conducting speedily the business for which they are created; and that the charge for the services rendered shall be no more than just and reasonable; and the Federal courts have not hesitated to determine what was a just and reasonable charge.

The courts hold that rates fixed by the State are *prima facie* reasonable, and while railway companies cannot be barred from showing the unremunerative character of such rates, they can only do so by disclosing—in addition to the cost of maintenance and operation—the exact cost of the plant employed, and that in arriving at such cost account can be taken only of monies actually expended in construction and equipment. Railway companies have evinced no desire to make disclosures of this character, although it would be easy in this way to show that the schedule of rates established by the State was unremunerative, if such was the case.

The cost of maintaining and operating any given railway is readily ascertainable, and it should be equally easy to determine its cost, but such a procedure is surrounded with grave difficulties—difficulties growing out of syndicates and construction companies, the manufacture of securities, of bond and stock waterings, the purchase and construction of branch lines at low cost and unloading upon the stockholders at high cost, stock and scrip dividends, bonus* of stock to purchaser of bonds, bonds sold to pay unearned dividends that much stock may be unloaded at high prices à la Wabash, the building of branch lines at low cost, capitalizing at high cost, and covering resulting profits into the treasury of the parent company to be distributed as dividends, and forever taxing the railway user to pay interest and dividends on the profits thus enjoyed, as well as by a thousand and one other shady devices by which water is added to the basic power of levying tolls and increasing the amount upon which the public is expected to furnish the means of paying interest and dividends.

The cost of the railway is known only to its managers, and rarely to them, as the constructors but seldom retain the management and railway accounts are manipulated in numberless peculiar ways for the sophistication of investors. For instance, on page 184 of the 1889 report of the Kansas Railroad Commissioners there is appended to the statement of bonded indebtedness, made by the Atchison, Topeka and Santa Fe, this note: "The early records of the Company are very incomplete and it is impossible to tell, with any accuracy, the amount realized from the issue of these bonds," i. e., $14,061,500 of first mortgage, land grant and consolidated bonds. Another typical case is that of a railway company in whose service was the writer, and which built a costly line of passenger steamers for lake service; but, by reason of the building of railways north and south of the lake, the operation of the line became unprofitable, the steamers were dismantled, engines sold and the great sum they represented dropped from the annual report of the company without a word of explanation.

Managers dealing thus with stockholders, are not likely to be more frank with the public. Indeed the cost of the railway, and the manipulations of such cost, are of the professional secrets which are employed to defraud railway users and investors, and a case or two in point may not be uninteresting, as showing some of the processes adopted in the manufacture and marketing of stocks and bonds, which are so frequently but evidences of corporate fraud, rather than ownership.

An illustration of the case with which investor and user are alike plundered is found in the case of a corporation controlling a valuable dividend-paying property, which another company parallels with expectation of profits only from construction, and by forcing a sale—eventually effected—to the older company, the result being the trebling of railway capital without an increase of traffic.

Another form of corporate fraud is the payment of unearned dividends from the proceeds of bonds sold, thus adding to the capitalization and necessitating the collection of unjust tolls to pay interest. These fraudulent payments are often made to enable the management to foist upon the public immense issues of worthless shares, such

*The Santa Fe and other companies have given as a bonus as much as ten shares of stock with each $1,000 bond sold.

dividends being continued as long as bonds can be sold and a market found for the stock, and when one of these bubbles is about to burst, the manipulators make further vast profits by selling "short" and then having disclosures made of the hopeless condition of the corporate finances.

Yet another form of corporate fraud is the purchase or construction of cheap branch lines, and selling them at two, three or four times their cost to the Company of whose interests the profiting parties are the trustees. Sometimes these lines are consolidated with that of the parent company and new issues of securities made to cover the added mileage, while in other cases the old company enables the schemers to sell immense issues of the shares and bonds of the auxiliary line at high prices by guaranteeing the bonds of the latter and leasing its road at an exorbitant rental. Loaded down in this way the old company frequently ceases to pay dividends.

Again the parent company resolves itself into a construction company and covers into its treasury the profits arising from the construction of cheap branches. For instance, it is shown on page 391 of the 1889 report of the Kansas Railroad Commissioners that the St. Louis & San Francisco Railway Company derived a profit of $67,871 from the construction of ten and one-half miles of road that should not have cost over $10,000 per mile, but which, with this profit added and stock issued for a nominal consideration, is capitalized for $28,845 per mile. This company has built many hundred miles in recent years, and construction profits have aided in the payment of dividends on preferred stock, while providing a basis for levying, for all time, tolls to pay interest and dividends on the bonds and stock representing the profits divided. Thus, the greater the profits from construction, the greater the sums which can hereafter be extorted from the user of the railway.

*Poor's Manual shows that to make contemplated extensions the stock of the Missouri Pacific was, during 1886-87, increased $15,000,000, and the funded debt $14,376,000, and while the capitalization of the parent company was thus increased $29,376,000,† the lines built or purchased were capitalized from $8,000 to $52,000 per mile, the result of such multiple capitalization being to add an immense amount of water to old as well as new issues. There are some very instructive phases of the construction of this new mileage. For instance, the 310 miles of the auxiliary Fort Scott, Wichita & Western is shown by Mr. Poor to have cost $4,666,000; the funded debt is shown by Kansas Railroad Commission to be $5,666,000, and Mr. Poor shows that $4,666,000 of such bonds are deposited with the Union Trust Company to secure $4,666,000 of Missouri Pacific trust mortgage bonds issued to provide the $4,666,000 which the road is said to have cost. Has the user of this railway a right to ask what became of the other $1,000,000 of mortgage bonds and the $7,000,000 of capital stock upon which rates are based, and which make up a capitalization of $8,000,000 in excess of cost, and what was the consideration therefor?

In the case of the 411 miles of the Missouri Pacific's Denver, Memphis & Atlantic line, Mr. Poor shows the cost to have been $4,920,000, and Kansas report shows bonded debt to be $6,561,000, the first mortgage bonds exceeding the cost by $1,641,000 and the entire capitalization being $8,202,000 in excess of cost, a large part of which was borne by the municipalities along the line. Like conditions obtain with all Missouri Pacific lines built of late years except two short ones not yet mortgaged.

Another mode of collecting excessive tolls and defrauding the public is that practiced by the subsidized Pacific lines in paying $900,000 per annum to the Pacific Mail Steamship Company to forego competition, and then charging the public two or three times this sum to recoup themselves for such illegal diversion of corporate funds.

A unique case is that of an Ohio corporation, where the men who afterwards became the directors and managers gave their notes to certain bankers for money borrowed for the purpose of buying the shares which were to give them control of the corporation, and, having by this means secured control, applied—in whole or in part—to the payment of such notes the first mortgage bonds of the company to the amount of $8,000,000, although

---

*"Poor's Manual" is a compendium of such financial and traffic statements as the railway companies prepare for publication.

†August, 1-90 - It is now stated that the Missouri Pacific has added $20,000,000 to its capitalization.

such bonds had, in compliance with the requirements of the statutes of Ohio, been issued for the express purpose of equipments, double tracks and other betterments.*

Many auxiliary lines have been built at costs ranging from $8,000 to $15,000 per mile, and capitalized at two, three, four, and even five times their cost, as in the case of the 107 miles of the Kansas Midland, costing, including a small equipment, but $10,200 per mile, of which 30 per cent. was furnished by the municipalities along its line; yet with construction profits and other devices this road shows a capitalization of $53,000 per mile.

Or take the 1,035 miles in Kansas of the Chicago, Kansas & Nebraska, built by the Chicago Rock Island & Pacific in much the same way and capitalized for $33,000 per mile. Kansas municipalities aided to the extent of $2,500 per mile in building this road, receiving the stock of the company in exchange for municipal bonds. Now, however, foreclosure proceedings are pending in the interest and at the procurement of the parent company (which owns, practically, all the bonds and stock of the auxiliary line except the stock issued to the municipalities) whereby the municipalities are to be despoiled of this $2,500,000.‡

This is no uncommon device for plundering the farmer and other tax-payers; and railway presidents, directors and managers, who would scorn to put their hands into the pocket of the farmer and abstract a (single) silver dollar, rarely hesitate when, by the devices described, they can take from the same farmer and his congeners a lump sum of $2,500,000, and the successful workers of such schemes, by one and the same act, acquire vast sums and a reputation for great financial ability.

Another type is found in the Marion & McPherson line of the Atchison, Topeka & Santa Fe,† built largely from old and much worn material, and originally capitalized for $28,000 per mile, being more than three times its cost. Under the recent re-organization of the Santa Fe each mile represents a much larger sum; but how much larger I am unable to ascertain from the accounting officers of that company, to whom application was made for definite information.

Other Santa Fe lines show peculiar phases of railway administration. For instance, the Santa Fe, jointly with the St. Louis & San Francisco, built the Wichita & Western, extending 125 miles through a sparsely settled district and not paying operating expenses; yet the Santa Fe, although having another and parallel line—the Southern Kansas—less than twenty-four miles south of the Wichita & Western, doubly paralleled itself by building a third line between the two, this third line, for one hundred miles, being eight to fourteen miles from the Wichita & Western on the north, and, for seventy miles, but ten to sixteen from the Southern Kansas on the south.

In this way has money been wasted in construction, the farmer unnecessarily burdened, the parent company loaded with an immense unproductive mileage, and rendered unable to pay fixed charges, and thousands of those investing in its securities reduced to sore straits, the reason for all of which is probably to be found in the profits—private or corporate—growing out of construction.

Perhaps the Santa Fe affords as fair an illustration as can be found of the ease with which twelve men, sitting in directors' chairs, can issue an edict for the creation of an hundred million or more of fiat property, the only evidence of the existence of which is found in reams of paper, and affording additional evidence of the great and growing utility of printer's ink as an instrument of advanced civilization. By this simple process, and without any addition to the property of the corporation, the liabilities of the Santa Fe have been increased more than $100,000,000, and while rates of interest may have been scaled down, the total of interest and principal have been scaled up. When an individual or firm fails creditors usually accept large reductions of principal in adjustment; but when a railway company like the Santa Fe fails they insist on doubling the principal and increasing the total of interest.

Although the earnings of the Santa Fe, in 1888, amounted to $2,944,529 less than operating expenses and fixed charges, the managers paid an unearned dividend of $2,625,-

*See the seventh annual report of the Columbus, Hocking Valley & Toledo Railway Company.
†Known as the "Atchison" in New England and as the "Santa Fe" in the West.
‡Since the publication of this article in the "Arena" the railway has been sold under decree of foreclosure and the municipalities deprived of their stock.

000, which, with other enormous additions to the liabilities, are to be an endless burden upon railway users and the warrant for the exaction of unjust tolls.

The Santa Fe's recently acquired control of the St. Louis & San Francisco lines—which are to be operated as a distinct property—is a remarkable instance of the that process of multiplying securities without the addition of a dollar's worth to the world's stock of property.

The St. Louis & San Francisco controlled 1,329* miles of railway, capitalized for the enormous sum of $70,402,800, being $52,200 per mile. The Santa Fe acquired control of this property by issuing $26,285,175 of new Santa Fe stock, not to retire the stock of the "Frisco," but to buy it and place it in the treasury of the Santa Fe and apply† such dividends as may accrue to the payment of current Santa Fe liabilities.

The result to the railway user will be that, whereas the "Frisco" property has been represented by $70,402,800 of "Frisco" and auxiliary stocks and bonds, it is now represented by that sum plus $26,285 175 of Santa Fe stock, which is an addition of fictitious capital upon which the user is expected to furnish revenue, and the owners of Santa Fe shares have that amount of water injected into their holdings.

†The Santa Fe holds 741,129½ shares, of the par value of $73,112,950, of stock of auxiliary lines built wholly from land grants, municipal aid, and proceeds of bonds sold, and for this immense number of shares the only consideration—as shown by the Santa Fe ledger—was $4,029, or a fraction over half of one cent a share. For 663,306½ of these shares, of the par value of $66,330,650, the only consideration shown is $15.00, being at the rate of 44.22 shares of the par value of $4,422.00 for one cent. Such is the stuff which passes current as railway securities and on which the railway user is taxed to pay dividends.

The Santa Fe affords a most instructive example of what may be accomplished in the way of multiplying securities by the hoodooing‡ of accounts, by reckless construction, the payment of stock dividends ($18,000,000), the giving of vast quantities of stock to the purchases of bonds, the payment of unearned dividends and the creation of $100,-000,000 and more of fiat securities at one or two sittings.

The seventy miles of the Columbus & Cincinnati Midland, built at a cost of about $17,000 per mile—of which some $1,500 per mile was donated by the people along its line —is capitalized at $57,000 per mile and earns nearly twelve per cent. on the money furnished by its builders, yet appears to earn but three per cent., while in its immense fictitious capital the foundation is laid for further exactions.

The enormous profits accruing from the operation of the construction company, and the unjust tax thereby forever imposed upon the public, is exemplified in the case of the "Credit Mobilier" and other construction devices connected with the building of the various Pacific lines, out of which grew no little corruption of legislators, the ruin, politically, of promising statesmen, and the amassing of so many great fortunes, typified in the case of the four men who built the Central Pacific and whose united worldly possessions in 1860 are said to have been but $120,000. Now, however, their estates are estimated at more than $120,000,000.

Mr. Poor states that "the cost per mile of the roads making returns (1888) as measured by the amount of their stocks and indebtedness equaled nearly $60,732 as against $58,603 for 1887," being an increase of $2,129 per mile, and at the price recently prevailing, it would require 135,000,000 bushels of the farmers' corn annually to pay 5 per cent. on the water absorbed by railway securities in one year, and by such waterings yearly it will take but fourteen years to absorb the entire corn crop to provide revenue on the added fluid. How long shall this process be permitted to continue?

Mr. Poor also states that, in the eleven central farming States, railway earnings have in eighteen years increased 175 per cent.; yet he forgets to tell us that such has been the shrinkage in the prices of farm products that the value of the wheat and corn crops in these States increased but 57 per cent., showing conclusively that the railways are

*Include such lines as the Kansas Midland, etc., built at costs ranging from $10,000 to $15,000 per mile.
†Financial Chronicle of May 31, 1890.
‡Poor's Manual, 1889, page 723.
§Ante, page 5.

taking a constantly increasing proportion of the proceeds arising from the sale of the products of the farm.

This is still more clearly shown on the same page in the statement that in these States railway revenue in 1870 was $12 for each unit of the population as against $18 in 1888. Thus the per capita transportation tax is shown to have increased 50 per cent.

Mr. Poor says: "With these facts before us, it is difficult to understand the extraordinary antipathy to railroad corporations in the West."

If such antipathy exists, probably Mr. Poor could understand it if he would but look at these facts, and others herein stated, in all their nakedness, keeping in view their true bearing upon the greatest of the nation's industries.

That no such antipathy exists is shown by the fact that, while the railways of Illinois are capitalized for $42,450 per mile, they are assessed for purposes of taxation at $7,863 per mile; those of Iowa are capitalized at $38,069, and assessed at $5,189; those of Nebraska are capitalized at $40,172, and assessed at $5,829, and those of Kansas are capitalized at $52,155, and assessed at $6,595 per mile.

We have seen some of the processes by which the investor is shorn and an enormous fictitious capitalization piled up to aid in taxing the farmer and others. Is it any wonder that when his wares are selling at starvation prices the farmer becomes restive under the burdens thus imposed and seeks to replace present ownership by that of the nation?

According to Mr. Poor, there existed 156,082 miles of railway at the close of 1888, showing a capitalization—including floating debts—of $9,367,398,954, to pay interest and dividends on which a toll is levied on all the industries of the country.

How much of this vast capitalization is real, and how much the fictitious outgrowth of the practices described?

Owing to the practices illustrated, it is impossible for railway companies to show the cost of their properties, and we are compelled to reach an approximation by estimating such cost, and thus determining the sum upon which revenue should accrue.

ESTIMATED COST PER MILE OF EXISTING RAILWAYS.

Grubbing and clearing	$ 100
Right of way and land damage	2,500
Earthwork and rock cuttings	4,500
Bridges, culverts and masonry	3 000
Ties—3,000	2,000
Rails, splices, bolts and spikes	4,000
Switches, side-tracks, cattle-guards, road crossings and fences	1,100
Track laying, surfacing and ballasting	2,300
Depots, water tanks, stock yards, shops and terminals	3,500
Equipment	4,500
Engineering, rents, interest, taxes and contingencies	2,700
Total cost per mile	$30,000

*That this estimate is more than ample is assured by the statement (in substance) of of Mr. H. V. Poor that the capitalization of the roads built from 1880 to 1883 is double the actual investment and, could the fictitious capital be eliminated, railways, as investments, would have no parallel; and in the statement that within five years ending in 1883, "about 40,000 miles of line were constructed at a cash cost of at least $1,100,000,000," being $27,000 per mile; and that "in 1884 only about 4,000 miles of new line were constructed, the cost of which did not exceed $20,000 per mile and perhaps not over $15,000 per mile."

For each mile of railway costing more than $30,000 per mile ten can be found that have cost from $8,000 to $20,000. The eastern two hundred miles of the Kansas division of the Union Pacific, built in the era of high prices, cost less than $20,000, although now bearing a capitalization of $105,000 per mile, but a well known manipulator—who made restitution of millions to the Erie—supervised its reorganization, which may account for the generous volume of water incorporated in its securities.

The Missouri Pacific line form El Dorado to McPherson, Kansas, a comparatively expensive prairie road, being located across the line of drainage, cost much less than $10,000 per mile, as have thousands of miles of other prairie lines.

*See Poor's Manual for 1881 and 1885.

Possibly $30,000 per mile is less than it would cost to duplicate the railways east of the Ohio, but the most of the mileage being west of that region, where the cost, outside of a few mountain roads, is at a minimum, the estimate, if erroneous, certainly errs in placing the cost too high. Moreover, we have a factor of safety in the fact that the nation, to aid in building railways, has granted 197,000,000 acres of land, a large part of which has passed into the possession of the railway companies, and from which they have realized vast sums, probably more than $300,000,000, to which should be added State and municipal aid and individual donations to the amount of $150,000,000 to $250,000,000.

Taking no account of the sums loaned the Pacific railways, the people have contributed at least $2,000 per mile towards the cost of existing railways, hence we are warranted in assuming that $30,000 per mile is the maximum sum on which the user should furnish revenue, less such revenue as the corporations derive from rents, interests and dividends, from lands, buildings, railways, stocks or bonds bought or brought into existence by an expenditure of any part of such $30,000 per mile or the earnings therefrom, such revenue, aside from traffic earnings, being now about $90,000,000 per annum.

It is claimed that in determining the amount of capital on which the rates of toll shall be based, the people are entitled to no voice, but as the compensation is to be reasonable and the measure of such compensation being the cost of maintaining and operating the railway plus a fair return for the capital actually employed, the people are unquestionably entitled to a voice in determining what such compensation shall be and how it shall be arrived at, and their representatives will find the railways have cost not to exceed an average of $30,000 per mile, and could be duplicated for enough less to more than offset the enhancement in the value of right of way, depot grounds and terminals.

Railways well located and mortgaged for 80 per cent. or less of actual cost can dispose of three and one-half to four and one-half per cent. bonds at par, but badly located or poorly managed roads often failing to pay interest, we may call five per cent. a fair rate, and on this basis the annual net revenue of roads existing at the close of 1888, from traffic, rents, interest, dividends and all other sources, should not exceed $234,123,000, being $67,408,000 less than the net traffic earnings reported by Poor, and taking the net earnings ($405,220,000) as shown by the Inter-State Commission, the excess is $171,097,000 wrongfully extorted from the agricultural and other industries in one year.

This difference in the amount of net earnings arises from the fact that, in Poor's Manual, only traffic earnings are tabulated,* no account being taken of the immense sums railway companies derive from rents of lands, buildings, track and terminals, as well as in the form of dividends on stocks and bonds owned, and the profits from the sale of such securities, all amounting to vast sums and yearly increasing as the railways become consolidated and absorb more and more of existing property; hence Mr. Poor's figures are incomplete and misleading, inasmuch as they fail to convey a correct idea of the total of railway earnings or the amount annually extorted from the user.

Of the $234,123,000 resulting from a five per cent. revenue on $30,000 per mile, a very large part, as will hereafter be shown, belongs to the user rather than the investor, while many parallel roads, built for construction profits, are needless, and others so badly located that the traffic will be wholly insufficient to provide revenue, and the owners must, like the owners of badly located buildings, suffer the loss entailed by lack of business sagacity. Favorably located roads can collect more than five per cent.; should they be permitted to do so? Each railway company is a distinct organization, each road a separate instrument and specially conditioned, and it is questionable if the compensation for the capital employed should, in any case, be permitted to exceed the rates fixed upon from time to time, as a just return. As interest rates fall, so should returns from railway investments.

Justice and reason appear to have little part in determining railway rates, the environments being all potent, as in the States where efficient granger laws† have been reinforced by a strong and active commission rates are much the lowest, and highest where

*Page 4 of the Introduction of Manual for 1889.
†"Granger laws" are the laws enacted in the agricultural States of the Mississippi Valley for the control of railway rates and methods.

either the laws or the commission are ineffecient; yet enough has been accomplished to show the beneficent possibilities of governmental control in suppressing some of the multifarious evil practices of railway companies, and while these practices continue they are much less common and not so flagrant as in the past, when the manager of an Inter. State railway, in order to destroy the value of the property of a coal company having no other outlet for its product, could, without a minute's notice, advance the rates on coal shipped by such company 133 per cent. above the rates charged another coal company in which such railway company and its officers were stockholders; nor, with the Inter-State law in force, are railway officials likely to repeat the indiscretion of such manager in writing the president of a coal company (of whose property he desired to force a sale) the subjoined letter:

St. Louis & San Francisco Railway Company,
Office of the Second Vice-President and General Manager,
St. Louis, Mo., February 9th, 1882.

President Pittsburg Coal Company, Pittsburg, Kansas:

DEAR SIR—I will pass through Pittsburg about 12 o'clock on Monday next, and would be glad to have you join me at Pittsburg, and go to Girard, and back to Pittsburg.

If we can buy your coal at a low price, I think we can possibly make a deal on that basis.

As long as you continue shipping coal, it has a demoralizing effect on the trade, *and renders the coal business unprofitable, to a certain extent, to the "ROGERS COAL COMPANY,"* Respectfully, C. W. ROGERS, *Second Vice-Pres't and Gen'l Manager.*

Discriminations and other fraudulent practices, whereby the few are enriched at the expense of the public, doubtless continue, and will until railway managers thus betraying their trusts are sent to keep company with the men who plundered the Ocean, Fidelity and Sixth Avenue banks; but there is, as compared with the time preceding the enactment of Inter-State and State laws, but little of the work of discrimination in progress; and great as is this evil, it is trivial as compared with those growing out of a capitalization excessive by more than one-half, and which is the warrant for annually levying an immense sum in unjust tolls, by which producer and consumer are alike despoiled of a large part of their earnings.

If the courts are right in holding that the carrier is entitled to but a reasonable compensation, and that the reasonableness of the charge rests upon the cost of maintenance, operation and the amount actually invested in the plant, then the exaction of existing rates of toll is wholly indefensible. As a bar to the rendering of justice to the user, the plea is made that should rates be reduced to what would afford but a fair return for the actual cost of the plant, it would work great hardships to the present holders of railway securities, who are assumed to have bought them in good faith, and many of whom are widows, orphans, trustees and institutions in which the poor have deposited their scanty savings. Has this plea against justice any basis except one of sentiment? If sentiment and a charitable regard for the poor and helpless shall govern, are there not twelve times as many widows orphans and poor among the 60,000,000 of railway users?

From the fact that there are 10,000 holders of New York Central stock, Mr. Poor estimates that there are 1,000,000 investors in railway securities, who, with their dependents, constitute a body of 5,000,000, and it is proposed that rather than this one-thirteenth shall surrender, once for all, so much of their power to tax others as is the direct product of fraud, they shall continue such unjust taxation.

This is not simply a proposition that one-thirteenth of the population shall unjustly tax all others this year, next year, or even the third or fourth year, but that such burden, yearly increasing by the addition of more water, shall be carried by the twelve-thirteenths to their graves; that when death relieves them, their children and children's children for countless generations, shall each in its turn take up the grievous burden and carry it until they also drop into the grave, and so long as these railways exist, this one-thirteenth shall possess the power to thus levy an iniquitous impost upon the entire industry of the country. Could anything be more unjust?

Shall 60,000,000 people and their descendants suffer a great and growing wrong rather than that 5,000,000 shall surrender a power to which they have no right?

The railway is public rather than private property, and while the stockholder is entitled to the usufruct and its limited control, yet such control is a trust for a specific purpose, such purpose being the service of the public, for which the compensation shall be just and reasonable, but the law never contemplated that one party in interest should alone be in possession of the knowledge necessary to a determination of the amount of capital employed and the reasonableness of the charges made, and so long as such knowledge is withheld shareholders must expect discontent on the part of the public and efforts to secure such control as will ensure justice; and it is this discontent which has been one of the most potent factors in bringing into existence the "Farmers' Alliance" and kindred organizations, in which millions of farmers—for the first time in history—are united for a common object.

The endowment of the railway company with the exceptional power to enter upon and take private property, and the equally exceptional limitation of the stockholders' liability to the cost of shares held, implies special duties and obligations to the public; and the people, whose lands have been taken, who furnish the traffic and provide the revenue, have a right to a voice in determining the justness of the rates charged.

Another plea is that the cost of transportation is less in the United States than elsewhere, hence there can be no cause of complaint. If rates are higher in Republican France or Imperial Germany, where railways exist, primarily, for military purposes, it is neither our duty to emulate them in such matters nor to copy their costly modes of railway administration; yet we may well profit by their example in providing for stringent control of railways and the rates for carriage.

The farmer, understanding that rates are unjust by reason of an enormous fictitious capitalization, and that such rates reduce the value of his land and its products, appeals to legislation for relief, which States have sought to furnish by laws regulating rates and methods of administration, which are denounced as acts of robbery by the men who have perpetrated the frauds of which such laws are the resultant.

The men loudest in denunciation of every attempt at control by law are those most active in the manufacture of securities, in operating the construction company, in paying unearned dividends, in selling or capitalizing cheap lines at many times their cost. These are the special champions of the widow, the orphan and the savings bank, whom they have despoiled by the most unblushing frauds. These are the innocent, chivalrous men, high in the esteem of the street and the exchange, who wish the way left open for more nickelplating, more Wabashing, more Credit Mobiliers and more stock and bond watering.

There is abundant evidence that where the laws have been such as to secure the greatest control—Illinois and Iowa—well located and judiciously managed railways are exceedingly prosperous. Many great lines derive the major part of their traffic from the granger States, yet the laws, which railway managers and investors denounce as acts of confiscation, have not prevented the payment of good dividends. Mr. Poor shows that, for twenty-five years, the Chicago & Alton dividends have averaged 8.7 per cent.; that the Chicago, Burlington & Quincy has paid regular cash dividends ranging from 8 to 10 per cent. per annum, and stock dividends aggregating $6,701,990. The Chicago, Rock Island & Pacific has done about as well in the way of dividends, although its traffic has been so largely drawn from Illinois and Iowa. Until certain bond and stock operations, the Chicago, Milwaukee & St. Paul paid 7 per cent. dividends, and the Chicago & Northwestern has swelled its capital account by the payment of stock dividends, while paying regular cash dividends of 6 to 8 per cent., and the Illinois Central has, for twenty-six years, paid dividends ranging from 4 to 10 per cent. per annum, and aggregating $56,989,847.

Notwithstanding these laws and that nearly or quite all these roads carry an undue amount of water, that crops have failed, and panics have prostrated the industries of the country, they have prospered, new lines been added from the tolls collected on the old, the investor received ample returns, and some of the managers enabled, by some occult process, to amass enormous fortunes, all going to show that the granger laws have not been oppressive, and that when railways fail to make fair returns it is due to faulty loca-

TABLE I.

Year.	Miles of railway in operation.	Capitalization per mile.	Net traffic earnings per Poor.	Net traffic earnings per mile.	Mileage on which investors are entitled to revenue.	Proportn of earnings p'r mile on road built by investors at cost of $30,000 per mile.	Proport'n of earnings p'r mile on fictitious capital.	EARNINGS OF FICTITIOUS CAPITAL AND MILES OF ROAD BUILT THEREFROM.			
								Earnings each y'r on fictitious capital.	Earnings of road built subsequent to 1871 from revenue furnished by railway users.	Tot'l earn'gs from fictitious capital and from capital and from milage built in preceding years from excessive tolls.	Miles of railway built in each y'r from capital tolls of fictit's capital and from tolls on milage built there.
1874	69,273	$59,256	$189,570,958	$2,736.57	69,273	$1,409.10	$1,327.47	$ 91,957,829		$ 91,957,829	3,065
1875	71,759	61,652	185,506,438	2,585.13	68,694	1,258.00	1,327.13	91,165,867	$ 7,923,423	99,089,290	3,303
1876	73,508	58,562	186,452,752	2,536.50	67,140	1,299.50	1,237.00	82,196,298	16,152,432	99,348,730	3,278
1877	74,112	60,678	170,976,607	2,307.00	64,466	1,142.00	1,165.00	75,074,930	22,306,690	97,383,620	3,246
1878	78,960	59,163	187,375,167	2,375.57	66,068	1,204.41	1,171.16	77,344,577	30,689,989	109,034,566	3,601
1879	79,009	57,730	216,544,599	2,740.76	62,516	1,424.10	1,316.66	82,276,706	45,277,355	127,554,121	4,251
1880	82,146	58,624	255,557,555	8,111.01	61,402	1,591.91	1,519.10	93,234,752	64,617,581	157,862,333	5,262
1881	92,971	60,445	272,406,787	2,330.02	66,965	1,455.02	1,475.00	98,733,550	74,277,210	175,010,760	5,534
1882	104,971	61,303	280,316,696	2,670.42	63,131	1,306.90	1,363.52	99,678,746	85,098,274	184,777,040	6,159
1883	110,414	62,030	293,367,285	2,656.07	72,415	1,295.54	1,370.53	99,209,924	100,999,717	200,209,643	6,674
1884	115,672	61,366	268,064,496	2,318.32	70,999	1,133.66	1,184.66	84,077,689	103,628,904	187,706,593	6,257
1885	123,320	61,398	260,493,931	2,185.32	72,390	1,067.75	1,117.57	80,870,718	111,357,351	192,228,069	6,408
1886	125,185	61,098	300,603,564	2,401.27	67,847	1,179.02	1,222.25	82,903,995	137,748,854	220,652,849	7,855
1887	137,029	58,603	334,989,119	2,444.67	72,395	1,251.67	1,198.00	86,263,444	155,219,042	244,482,486	8,149
1888	145,387	60,731	301,731,051	2,074.61	72,545	1,024.86	1,019.75	86,125,770	131,174,756	237,300,526	7,910
Totals...								$1,311,114,857	$1,111,473,578	$2,422,588,455	84,752

The above computations are based on a cost of $30,000 per mile, and the unwarranted assumption that investors furnished the money to build all the roads existing in 1874.

TABLE II.

Showing revenue of investors at six per cent. on cost of $30,000 per mile and mileage built from earnings in excess of six per cent.

Years.	Miles of railway in operation.	Mileage on which investors' revenue is computed.	Capital furnished by investors on the basis of cost being $30,00 per mile.	Revenue of investors on basis of six per cent. on cost of $30,000 per mile.	Revenue of railways from traffic earnings, Per Poor.	Earnings in excess of six per cent. on $30,000 per mile, hence belonging to the railway user, but employed in building new roads.	Miles of railway built from tolls in excess of six per cent. on $37,00 per mile, and to the revenue from which investor has no right.
1874	69,273	69,273	$2,078,190,000	$124,961,400	$189,570,958	$ 64,879,558	2,163
1875	71,759	69,506	5,087,880,000	125,272,800	185,506,438	60,233,638	2,008
1876	73,508	69,337	2,080,110,000	124,806,600	185,452,752	62,646,152	2,039
1877	74,112	67,853	2,035,590,000	122,135,400	170,976,697	48,841,297	1,628
1878	78,960	71,073	2,132,190,000	127,931,400	187,575,167	59,643,767	1,988
1879	79,009	69,134	2,074,020,000	124,441,200	216,544,999	92,103,779	3,070
1880	82,146	69,301	2,076,030,000	124,561,800	235,557,555	130,995,755	4,366
1881	92,971	75,660	2,269,800,000	136,188,000	272,406,787	136,218,787	4,541
1882	104,971	82,119	2,493,570,000	149,614,200	280,316,696	130,702,496	4,357
1883	110,414	84,205	2,526,150,000	151,569,000	293,367,285	141,798,285	4,726
1884	115,672	84,737	2,542,110,000	152,526,600	269,064,496	115,537,896	3,851
1885	123,320	88,524	2,655,720,000	159,343,200	269,493,931	110,150,731	3,672
1886	125,185	86,727	2,601,810,000	156,108,600	300,603,564	144,494,900	4,816
1887	137,028	93,751	2,812,620,000	168,757,200	334,989,119	166,231,919	5,542
1888	143,387	96,572	2,897,160,000	173,829,600	301,631,051	127,801,451	4,260
Totals					$1,592,280,471		52,076

tion, unreasonable rate wars, speculative or incompetent management or an extraordinary excess of water in capitalization.

Possibly a flood of light may be thrown on this subject by the experience of the writer when general freight and passenger agent of a new railway. Imbued with the idea that the prosperity of the road would be subserved by encouraging immigration and fostering business, the writer formulated tariffs calculated to further such ends. Imagine his astonishment when told by the general manager they would not answer, and to be informed that the road was not being built to make money out of its operation, but out of its construction, and what was required of the traffic department was the greatest present revenue possible and to make the passenger rates just low enough to take the traffic from the stages and the freight rates no lower than necessary to drive the ox teams out of the freight business.

The policy then outlined was pursued until the railway passed through the reorganization thereby made inevitable, and this cheaply-built prairie line, with free right of way and land grant and subsidy equal to its entire cost, is now capitalized for $105,000 per mile.

On most railways the basic principle underlying tariff and schedule is "All the traffic will bear," and it is to hold in check these "Chevaliers of the road" that granger laws are formulated.

It may be safely assumed that $30,000 per mile is the outside cost of existing railways, and the aggregate, at the close of 1888, on which tolls should be based, was $4,682,-246,000; but here the question arises: How much of this sum has the railway builder furnished, and what part has been extorted from the railway user in the form of excessive tolls?

Available data does not admit of going back of 1874, when 69,273 miles were in operation, the cost of which, at $30,000 per mile, being credited to the builders; and adopting the net (traffic) earnings as shown by Poor we find that, in 1874, crediting each $30,000 with its proportion of such earnings, pro rata—and adopting the capitalists' theory that the water in the capital is entitled to the same revenue as the money part thereof —the earnings of the water in the capitalization of that year amounted to $91,957,829, being equal to the cost of 3,065 miles of railway. Continuing such computations for fourteen years and crediting the railway users with the income of so much of the railway mileage as was, from year to year, built from the tolls collected on the capitalization in excess of $30,000 per mile, it appears that the users have, within fifteen years, been mulcted, in the shape of tolls based wholly on water, in the sum of *$2,422,588,455, from which those in possession have constructed 80,752 miles of new railway, leaving but 2,901 miles, costing $87,030,000, to have been built, in the same period, from funds supplied by those claiming to own all the railways. For details of these computations see Table I.

Should it be claimed that instead of dividing the earnings pro rata between the real and fictitious capital, that the real is entitled to full compensation before anything is assigned to the fictitious, we will, without admitting that the preceding computations are not correctly based, proceed to first give compensation, at the rate of six per cent. per annum, for all the capital actually employed (except that furnished by the users in the form of tolls in excess of such six per cent.), and again assuming that the capital to build all the roads existing in 1874 had been furnished by the putative owners, and we find the results as set forth in table II.

Table II shows that from traffic earnings alone the holders of shares and bonds have received six per cent. per annum for every dollar invested and have, within fifteen years, been enabled, by the watery fiction, to extort from railway users the enormous sum of $1,592,280,471 (to which should be added about half as much more from miscellaneous earnings), with which has been built 53,076 miles of railway, for the use of which it is proposed to forever tax those who have furnished all the money employed in its construction.

Is it possible that no remedy can be found for such evils? In the National Bank the law has created another form of public trust, but one whose relations to the people

*This is from traffic earnings alone, to which should be added a vast sum from miscellaneous sources.

are infinitely less intimate and with the services of which the public could dispense without serious results.

The railway and the bank each perform functions that the State might; yet the bank alone is held to the most rigid discharge of its duties, a maximum fixed for its rates of toll, the amount it shall loan any one party, and the kind of security determined as well as the amount of its reserve fund, its books and assets at all times subject to inspection without notice, no share issued until paid for in full, the payment of unearned dividends made a penal offense and breaches of trust punished in an exemplary manner.

Can there be any sufficient reason why the railway corporation, with infinitely greater power and privileges, performing functions a thousand times more important, and directly affecting a hundred persons for one affected by bank administration, should not be subjected to control quite as stringent and quite as far-reaching?

Shares and bonds being the basis of tolls, should a railway company be permitted to issue share or bond until its par value in actual money has been covered into the corporate treasury?

Should the basis of tolls be laid until it has been shown that a proposed line is necessary to public convenience and will make fair returns on its cost?

Should a railway company be permitted to collect tolls until it has shown the exact cost of the instrument of transportation?

Should it not be a penal offense for a railway official to pay an unearned dividend?

Should not railway accounts, stock and bond ledgers and assets be subjected to like inspection as those of national banks?

Would not rate wars cease were railways, once having reduced rates, debarred from ever again advancing them without governmental permission?

Should not railway companies be taxed on their capitalization as shown in issues of bonds and shares?

Should not railways be appraised at present cash value, and earnings from all sources, be limited to what would afford a given maximum return on such appraisal?

Or should the nation assume the ownership and operate the railways through a non-partisan commission, as the Province of Victoria, Australia, has shown to be both practical and economical?

There is no longer any question as to the power of the nation to control these great arteries of trade, nor is there outside a limited circle, any question as to the necessity of such control, and it but remains for the lawgivers to formulate such statutes as will protect user and investor, both of whom are at the mercy of a small body of men who can and do make and mar the fortunes of individuals, cities and States without let or hindrance

*SHOULD THE NATION OWN THE RAILWAY?

When the paper published in the February *Arena*, entitled "The Farmer, the Investor and the Railway," was written the writer was not ready to accept national ownership as a solution of the railway problem, but the occurrences attending the flurries of last Autumn in the money markets, when half a dozen men, in order to obtain control of certain railways, entered into a conspiracy that came near wrecking the entire industrial and commercial interests of the country, having shed a lurid light upon the enormous and baleful power which the corporate control of the railways places in the hands of what Theodore Roosevelt aptly termed "the dangerous wealthy classes," has had the effect of converting to the advocacy of national ownership, not only the writer, but vast numbers of conservative people of the Central, Western and Southern States, to whom

*First published in the *Arena* July and August, 1891.

the question now assumes this form: "Which is to be preferred, a master in the shape of a political party that it is possible to dislodge by the use of the ballot or one in the shape of ten or twenty Goulds, Vanderbilts, Huntingtons, Rockefellers, Sages, Dillons and Brices who never die and whom it will be impossible to dislodge by the use of the ballot?" The particular Gould or Vanderbilt may die, as did that Vanderbilt to whom is ascribed the aphorism "The public be damned," but the spirit and power of the Goulds and Vanderbilts never die.

OBJECTIONS TO NATIONAL OWNERSHIP.

The objections to national ownership are many; that most frequently advanced and having the most force being the possibilty that, by reason of its control of a vastly increased number of civil servants, the party in possession of the federal administration at the time such ownership was assumed would be able to perpetuate its power indefinitely. As there are more than 700,000 people employed by the railways this objection would seem to be well taken, and it indicates serious and far-reaching results, *unless* some way can be devised to neutralize the political power of such a vast addition to the official army.

In the military service we have a body of men that exerts little or no political power, as the moment a citizen enters the army he divests himself of political functions, and it is not hazardous to say that 700,000 capable and efficient men can be found who, for the sake of employment to be continued so long as they are capable and well-behaved, will forego the right to take part in political affairs. If a sufficient number of such men can be found this objection would, by proper legislation, be divested of all its force. At all events, no trouble from such a source has been experienced since Australian railways were placed under control of non-partisan commissions, such commissions having had charge of the Victorian railways since February, 1884, or a little more than one term, they having been appointed for seven years, instead of for life, as stated by Mr. W. M. Acworth in his argument against government control in the March *Forum.*

The second objection is that there would be a constant political pressure to make places for the strikers of the party in power, thus adding a vast number of useless men to the force and rendering it progressively more difficult to effect a change in the political complexion of the administration.

That this objection has much less force than is claimed is clear from the conduct of the Postal Department, which is unquestionably a political adjunct to the administration; yet but few useless men are employed, while its conduct of the mail service is a model of efficiency after which the corporate managed railways might well pattern. Moreover, if the railways are put under non-partisan control this objection will lose nearly if not quite all its force.

A third objection is that the service would be less efficient and cost more than with continued corporate ownership.

This appears to be bare assertion, as from the very nature of the case there can be no data outside that furnished by the government-owned railways of British colonies, and such data negatives these assertions and the advocates of national ownership are justified in asserting that such ownership would materially lessen the cost. Any expert can readily point out many ways in which the enormous costs of corporate management would be lessened. With those familiar with present methods and not interested in their perpetuation, this objection has no force whatever.

The fourth objection is that with constant political pressure unnecessary lines would be built for political ends.

This is also bare assertion, although it is not impossible that such results would follow; yet such has not been the case in the British colonies, where the governments have had control of construction. On the other hand, it is notorious that under corporate ownership, and solely to reap the profits to be made out of construction, the United States have been burthened with useless parallel roads and such corporations as the Santa Fe have paralled their own lines for such profits. It is quite safe to say that when the nation owns the railways there will be no nickelplating, nor will such an unnecessary expenditure be made as was involved in the construction of the West Shore; nor will the feat of

Gould and the Santa Fe be repeated of building 240 miles side by side for construction profits, much of which is located in the arid portion of Kansas, where there is never likely to be traffic for even one railway. Much of the Republic is covered with closely parallel lines which would never have been built under national ownership, and this process will continue as long as the manipulators can make vast sums out of construction.

A fifth objection is that with the amount of red-tape that will be in use it will be impossible to secure the building of needed lines.

While such objection is inconsistent with the fourth, it may have some force, but as the greater part of the country is already provided with all the railways that will be needed for a generation it is not a very serious objection, even if it is as difficult as asserted to procure the building of new lines. It is not probable, however, that the government would refuse to build any line that would clearly subserve public convenience; the conduct of the postal service negativing such a supposition, and for party purposes the administration would certainly favor the construction of such lines as were clearly needed and it is high time that only such should be built, and what instrumentality so fit to determine this as a non-partisan commission acting as the agent of the whole people? The sixth objection is that lines built by the government would cost much more than if built by corporations.

Possibly this would be true, but they would be much better built and cost far less for maintenance and "betterments" and would represent no more than actual cost, and such lines as the Kansas Midland, costing but $10,200 per mile, would not, as now, be capitalized at $53,024 per mile, nor would the president of the Union Pacific (as does Sidney Dillon in the *North American Review* for April) say that "A citizen, simply as a citizen, commits an impertinence when he questions the right of a corporation to capitalize its properties at any sum whatever," as then there would be no Sidney Dillons who would be presidents of corporations pretending to own railways built wholly from government moneys and lands, and who have never invested a dollar in the construction of a property which they have now capitalized at the modest sum of $106,000 per mile. After such an achievement in making much out of nothing, it is no wonder that Mr. Dillon is a multi-millionaire and thinks it an impertinence when a citizen asks how he has discharged his trust in relation to a railway built wholly with public funds, no part of which Mr. Dillon and his associates seem in haste to pay back; their indebtedness to the government, with many years of unpaid interest, amounting to more than $50,000,000, which is more than the cash cost of the railway upon which these men have been so sharp as to induce the government, after furnishing all the money expended in its construction, to accept a second mortgage, and now asks the same accommodating government to reduce the rate of interest—which they make no pretense of paying—to a nominal figure, and to wait another hundred years for both principal and interest. To make sure that the government's second mortgage shall be no more valuable than second mortgages usually are, and to make it more comfortable for the manipulators, Messrs. Gould and Dillon now propose to put a blanket first mortgage of $250,000,000 on this property built wholly from funds derived from the sale of government lands and bonds, and to pay the interest on which bonds the people are yearly taxed, although Mr. Dillon and his associates contracted to pay such interest. In his conception of the relations of the railway corporations to the public Mr. Dillon is clearly not in accord with the higher tribunals which hold, in substance, that railways are public rather than private property and that the share-holders are entitled to but a reasonable compensation for the capital actually expended in construction and a limited control of the property and in this connection it may be well to quote briefly from decisions of the United States Supreme Court, which, in the case of the Wabash Railway vs. Illinois, uses this language: "The highways in the state are the highways of the state. The highways are not of private but of public institution and regulation. In modern times, it is true, government is in the habit, in some countries, of letting out the construction of important highways, requiring a large expenditure of capital, to agents generally corporate bodies created for the purpose, and giving them the right of taxing those who travel or transport goods thereon as a means of obtaining compensation for their outlay; but a superintending power over the highways and the charges imposed upon the public for their use always remains in the government." Again in Olcott vs. the Supervisors it is held that: "Whether the use of a railway is a public or private one depends in no measure upon the question who constructed it or who owns it. It has never been considered of any importance that the road was built by the agency of a private corporation. No matter who is the agent the function performed is that of the State."

Mr. Justice Bradley says: "When a railroad is chartered it is for the purpose of performing a duty which belongs to the State itself.   *   *   *   *   It is the duty and prerogative of the State to provide means of intercommunication between one part of its territory and another."

If, as appears, such is the duty of the State (nation) why should not the State resume the discharge of this duty when the corporate agents to which it has delegated it are found to be using the delegated power for the purpose of oppressing and plundering a public which it is the duty of the government to protect?

The abilities of the man who cannot become a multi-millionaire with the free use, for 25 years, of $33.000,000 of government funds must be of a very low order and it is no wonder, that after having for so many years had the use of such a sum without payment of interest Mr. Dillon and his associates are very wealthy and like others who are retaining what does not belong to them think it an impertinence when the owner enquires what use they are making of property to which they have no right. Had the nation built the Union Pacific there would have been no "Credit-Mobilier" and its unsavory scandal and it is safe to say that the road would not now be made to represent an expenditure of $106,000 per mile and that Mr. Dillon and some others would not have so much money as to warrant them in putting on such insufferable airs. When it is remembered what use Oaks Ames and the Union Pacific crew made of issues of stock it is not at all surprising that the president of the Union Pacific should think it an impertinence for a citizen to question the amount of capitalization or the use to which a part of such issues have been put some of which are within the knowledge of the writer so far as relates to issues of that part of the Union Pacific lying in Kansas and built by Samuel Hallett who told the writer that he gave a member of the then federal cabinet several thousand shares of the capital stock of the "Union Pacific Railway Eastern Division"—now the Kansas division of the Union Pacific—to secure the acceptance of sections of the road which were not built in accordance with the requirements of the act of Congress which provided that a given amount of government bonds per mile should be delivered to the railway company when certain officials should accept the road and it was a quarrel with the chief engineer of the road in relation to a letter written by such engineer to President Lincoln, informing him of the defective construction of this road, that caused Samuel Hallett to be shot down in the streets of Wyandotte, Kansas by engineer Talcott. It is within the the knowledge of the writer that the member of the cabinet to whom Mr. Hallett said he gave several thousand shares of stock held an amount of Union Pacific shares years afterwards and that many years after he left the cabinet he continued to draw a large salary from the Union Pacific company. Mr. Hallett also told the writer the arguments applied to Congressmen to induce them to change the government lien from a first to a second mortgage of the Pacific Railway lines and what was his contribution in dollars to the fund used to enable congressmen to see the force of the arguments used.

When issues of railway shares are used for corrupt purposes it is certainly an impertinence for a citizen to make enquiries or offer any remarks in relation thereto.

The seventh objection to state owned railways is that they are incapable of progressive improvement, as are corporate owned ones, and will not keep pace with the progress of the nation in other respects, and in his *Forum* article Mr. Acworth lays great stress upon this phase of the question and argues that as a result the service will be far less satisfactory than now.

There may be force in this objection, but the evidence points to the opposite conclusion. When the nation owns the railways trains will run into union depots, the equipment will become uniform and of the best character, and so sufficient that the traffic of no part of the country would have to wait while the worthless locomotives of some bankrupt corporation were being patched up, nor would there be the present difficulties in obtaining freight cars, growing out of the poverty of corporations which have been plundered by the manipulators, nor would improvement be hindered by the diverse ideas of the managers of various lines in relation to the adoption of devices intended to render life more secure, or to add to the public convenience. That such is one of the evils of corporate management is demonstrated daily and is shown by the following from the *Railway Review* of March 7th, 1891: "It is stated that a bill will be introduced in the Illinois legislature, at the suggestion of the railroad and warehouse commissioners, governing the placing of interlocking plants at railway grade crossings. It sometimes happens that one of the companies concerned is anxious to put in such a plant and the other objects. At present there is no law to govern the matter and the enterprising company is forced to abide the time of the other." Instead of national ownership being a hindrance to improvement and enterprise the results in Australia prove the contrary, as in Victoria the government railways are already provided with interlocking plants at all grade crossings and one line does not have to wait the motion of another, but all are governed by an active and enlightened policy which adopts all beneficial improvements, appliances or modes of administration that will add either to the public safety, comfort or convenience. It is safe to say that had the nation been operating the railways there would have been no Fourth avenue tunnel horror and Chauncy Depew and associates would not now be under indictment, as the government would not have continued the use of the death dealing stove on half the railways in the country in order to save money for the shareholders.

Existing evidence all negatives Mr. Acworth's postulate "That state railway systems are incapable of vigorous life."

An objection to national ownership which the writer has not seen advanced is that states, counties, cities, townships and school-districts would loose some $27,000,000 of revenue derived from taxes upon railways.

While this would be a serious loss to some communities there would be compensating advantages for the public as the cost of transportation would be lessened in like measure.

Many believe stringent laws enforced by commissions having judicial powers will serve the desired end and the writer was long hopeful of the efficacy of regulation by state and national commissions but close observation of their endeavors and of the constant efforts—too often successful—of the corporations to place their tools on such commissions and to evade all laws and regulations have convinced him that such control is and must continue to be ineffective and that the only hope of just and impartial treatment for railway users is to exercise the "right of eminent domain", condemn the railways and pay their owners what it would cost to duplicate them and in this connection it may be well to state what valuations some of the corporations place upon their properties.

Some years since the "Santa Fe" filed in the counties on its line a statement showing that at the then price of labor and materials—rails were then double the present price—that the road could be duplicated for $9,695 per mile and the materials being badly worn the actual cash value of the road did not exceed $7,725 per mile.

In 1885 the superintendent of the St. Louis & Iron Mountain Railway, before the Arkansas State Board of Assessors, swore that he could duplicate such railway for $11,000 per mile and yet Mr. Gould has managed to float its securities notwithstanding a capitalization of five times that amount.

THE ADVANTAGE OF NATIONAL OWNERSHIP.

First would be the stability and practical uniformity of rates now impossible, as they are subject to change by hundreds of officials, and are often made for the purpose of enriching such officials. State and federal laws have had the effect of making discriminations less public and less numerous, but it is doubtful if they are less effective in enriching officials and their partners although it may be necessary to be more careful in covering up tracks. That they are continued is within the cognizance of every well in. formed shipper and are made clear by such cases as that of Counselman and Peasley now before the United States Supreme Court. Conselman and Peasley—one a large shipper and the other a prominent railway official—refused to testify before a United States grand jury upon the plea that to do so might criminate themselves; the federal law making it a criminal offense to make or benefit by discriminating rates. Counselman had been given rates on corn some five cents less per 100 pounds than others from Kansas and Nebraska points to Chicago.

The outrageous character of this discrimination will appear when we reflect that five cents per 100 pounds is an enormous profit on corn that the grower has sold at from 18 to 20 cents per 100 pounds and that such a margin would tend to drive every one but the railway officials and their secret partners out of the trade, as has practically been the case on many western roads. Doubtless such rates are sometimes made in order to take the commodity over a certain line, and there is no divide with the officials; but the effect upon the competitors of the favored shipper and the public is none the less injurious and such practices would not obtain under national ownership, when railway users would be treated with honesty and impartiality which the experience of half a century shows to be impossible with corporate ownership.

Referring to the rate question in their last report the Interstate Commerce Commission says: "If we go no farther than the railroad managers themselves for information, we shall not find that it is claimed that railroad service, as a whole, is conducted without unjust discrimination."

"If rates are secretly out, or if rebates are given to large shippers, the fact of itself shows the rates which are charged to the general public are unreasonable, for they are necessarily made higher than they ought to be in order to provide for the cut or to pay the rebate."

"If the carrier habitually carries a great number of people free, its regular rates are made the higher to cover the cost; if heavy commissions are paid for obtaining business, the rates are made the higher that the net revenues may not suffer in consequence; if scalpers are directly or indirectly supported by the railroad companies, the general public refunds to the companies what the support costs."

The commission quote a Chicago railway manager as saying: "Rates are absolutely demoralized and neither shippers, passengers, railways, or the public in general make anything by this state of affairs. Take passenger rates for instance; they are very low; but who benefits by the reduction? No one but the scalpers. * * * * In freight matters the case is just the same. Certain shippers are allowed heavy rebates, while others are made to pay full rates. * * * * The management is dishonest on all sides, and there is not a road in the country that can be accused of living up to the interstate law. Of course when some poor devil comes along and wants a pass to save him from starvation he has several clauses of the interstate act read to him; but when a rich shipper wants a pass, why he gets it at once."

From years of ineffectual efforts, on the part of state and national legislatures and commissions, to regulate the rate business it would appear that the only remedy is national ownership, which would place the rate making power in one body, with no induce. ment to act otherwise than fairly and impartially, and this would simplify the whole business and relegate an army of traffic managers, general freight agents, soliciting agents, brokers, scalpers, and hordes of traffic association officials to more useful callings while relieving the honest user of the railway of intolerable burthens.

Under corporate control, railways and their officials have taken possession of the majority of the mines which furnish the fuel so necessary to domestic and industrial life, and there are but few coal fields where they do not fix the price at which so essential an article shall be sold, and the whole nation is thus forced to pay undue tribute.

Controlling rates and the distribution of cars, railway officials have driven nearly all the mine owners to the wall who have not railways or railway officials for partners. For instance; in Eastern Kansas, on the line of the "St. Louis & San Francisco Railway

Company," were two coal companies, whose plants were of about equal capacity, and several individual shippers. The railway company and its officials became interested in one of the coal companies and such company was, by the rebate and other processes, given rates which averaged but forty per cent. of the rates charged other shippers the result being that all the other shippers were driven out of the business, a part of them being hopelessly ruined before giving up the struggle. In addition to gross discriminations in rates this railway company practiced worse discriminations in the distribution of cars; for instance during one period of 564 days, as was proven in court, they delivered to the Pittsburg Coal Company 2371 empty cars to be loaded with coal although such company had sale for and a capacity to produce and load, during the same period, more than 15,000 cars. During the same period the railway company delivered to the "Rogers Coal Company" in which the railway company and C. W. Rogers, its vice president and general manager, were interested, no less than 15,483 coal cars while 456 were delivered to individual shippers. In other words; the coal company owned, in large part, by the railway and its officials, was given 82 per cent. of all the facilities to get coal to market, although the other shippers had much greater combined capacity than had the Rogers Coal Company.

During the last four months of the period named, and when the Pittsburg Coal Company had the plant, force and capacity to load thirty cars per day, they received an average of one and a fourth cars per day, resulting, as was intended, in the utter ruin of a prosperous business and the involuntary sale of the property, while the railway coal company, the railway officials, and the accommodating friends who operated the Rogers Coal Company made vast sums of money, and when all other shippers had thus been driven off the line the price of coal was advanced to the consumer.

On another railway, traversing the same coal field, the railway or its officials became interested in the Keith & Perry Coal Company—the largest coal company doing business on the line—and here the plan seems to have been, in addition to the manipulation of rates, to starve other mine operators out, and force them to sell their coal to the Keith & Perry company, by failing to furnish the needed cars to those who did not sell their coal to the Keith & Perry company at a very low price.

When the Keith & Perry company had a great demand for coal, such parties as sold the product of their mines to that company were furnished with cars, but for the other operators cars were not to be had, such cars as were brought to the field being assigned to such parties as were loading to the Keith & Perry company, the plea being that such company furnished the coal consumed by the locomotives of the railway.

One operator, after being for years forced in this way to sell his product to the Keith & Perry company or see his several plants stand idle, has, in recent months, been obliged to build some seven miles of railway in order to reach four different roads and thus have a fighting chance for cars, although all these railways are provided with coal mines owned by the corporations or their officials.

In Arkansas Jay Gould, or his railway company, own coal mines and the coal is transported to the neighboring town at low rates and there is an ample supply of cars for such mines, but the owners of an adjoining mine are forced to haul their coal, some eighteen miles, to the same town in wagons, as the rates charged them over Mr. Gould's railway are so high as to absorb the value of the coal at destination.

Not only are individuals thus oppressed, but for reasons which only the initiated can fathom there are seemingly purposeless discrimination against localities, as shown in the following extract from the *Coal Trade Journal* of March 25th, 1891:

"Capt, Thomas H. Bates, before the railroad committee of the Colorado Senate said: The Grand River Coal and Coke Company mine their coal in Garfield County, about fifty miles west of Leadville, and all they sell in Denver, Colorado Springs and Pueblo, has to be hauled through Leadville. At Leadville the individual consumer has to pay seven dollars per ton for this coal while in Denver, with an additional haul of 150 miles, the coal from the same mines is delivered to the individual consumer for $5.50 per ton. The Colorado Coal & Iron Company produce all the anthracite coal sold in Colorado. It is mined at Crested Butte, which is 150 miles nearer Leadville than

Denver yet this coal is sold in Leadville for $9.00 to the individual consumer while the same coal is hauled 150 miles farther and sold to the individual consumer for an advance of 25 cents per ton over the Leadville price and is sold in Denver for $7.10 per ton in carload lots."

With the government operating the railways, discriminations would cease, as would individual and local oppression; and we may be sure that an instant and absolute divorce would be decreed between railways and their officials on one side and commercial enterprises of every name and kind on the other.

There are but three countries of any importance where the railways are operated by corporations permitted to fix rates as in all others the government is the ultimate rate making power; these are Great Britain, Canada, and the United States, and while the British government exercises a more effective control than we do there are many and oppressive discriminations, and complaints loud and frequent and English farmers find it necessary to unite for the purpose of securing protection from corporate oppression as is shown by the following from the *Liverpool Courier* of January 29th, 1891.

"LANCASHIRE FARMERS AND RAILWAY RATES.

"After the counsel given them yesterday by Mr. A. B. Forwood of Ormskirk, it may be expected that the Liverpool District Farmers' Club will be on the watch for tangible evidence of their grievances against the railway companies.   *   *   *   *   *   Under certain circumstances competition operates to the advantage of the public, and rival carriers are constrained to convey goods from place to place at moderate charges, but where a company is not held in check the tendency is for rates to advance. In many cases, too, special interests of the companies are promoted at the expense of localities, and even individuals are subjected to the wrong of preferential charges. (There are no complaints in Britain that these discriminations are practised for the purpose of enriching the officials.) Hence the necessity for the Railway Commission to regulate the magnates of the iron road, who, when left without restraint pay little regard to interests other than those of their share-holders."

Although Mr. Acworth fails to mention this phase of English railway administration it would appear that the evils of discrimination are common under corporate management in Great Britain and that they are inherent to and inseparable from such management, and that the questions of rates, discriminations and free traffic in fuel can be satisfactorily adjusted only by national ownership and if for no other reasons such ownership is greatly to be desired.

The failure to furnish equipment to do the business of the tributary country promptly is one of the greater evils of corporate administration, enabling officials to practice most injurious and oppressive forms of discrimination and is one that neither federal or state commission pays any attention to. With national ownership a sufficiency of cars would be provided. On many roads the funds that should have been devoted to furnishing the needed equipment, and which the corporations contracted to provide when they accepted their charters, have been divided as construction profits, or, as in the case of the Santa Fe, Union Pacific and many others, diverted to the payment of unearned dividends while the public suffers from this failure to comply with charter obligations; yet, Mr. Dillon informs us that the citizen commits an impertinence when he enquires why contract obligations, which are the express consideration for the exceptional powers granted, are not performed.

Another great advantage which would result from national ownership would be such an adjustment of rates that traffic would take the short route and not, as under corporate management, be sent around by way of Robin Hood's barn, when it might reach destination by a route but two-thirds as long, and thus saving the unnecessary tax to which the industries of the country are subjected. That traffic can be sent by these round-about routes at the same or less rates than is charged by the shorter ones is *prima facie* evidence that rates are too high. If it costs a given sum to transport a specific amount of merchandise a thousand miles, it is clear that it will cost a greater sum to transport it fifteen hundred; and yet traffic is daily diverted from the thousand mile route to the fifteen hundred one and carried at the same or lower rates than is charged by the shorter line. It is evident that if the long route can afford to do the business for the rates charged that the rates charged by the shorter are excessive in a high degree.

Under government management traffic would take the direct route, as mail matter now does, and the industries of the country be relieved of the enormous tax imposed by needless hauls. Only those somewhat familiar with the extent of the diversions from direct routes can form any conception of the aggregate saving that would be effected by such change as would result from national ownership, and which may safely be estimated as equal to 2½ per cent. of the entire cost of the railway service, or $25,000,000 per annum.

With the government operating the railways there would be a great reduction in the number of men employed in towns entered by more than one line. For instance take a town where there are three or more railways and we find three (or more) full fledged staffs, three (or more) expensive up-town freight and ticket offices, three (or more) separate sets of all kinds of officials and employes, and three (or more) separate depots and yards to be maintained.

Under government control these staffs—except in very large cities—would be reduced to one, and all trains would run into one centrally located depot; freight and passengers be transferred without present cost, annoyance and friction, and public convenience and comfort subserved and added to in manner and degree almost inconceivable.

Economies which would be effected by such staff reductions would more than offset any additions to the force likely to be made at the instance of politicians, thus eliminating that objection, and such saving may be safely estimated at $20,000,000 per annum.

With the nation owning the railways the great number of expensive attorneys now employed, with all the attendant corruption of the fountains of Justice, can be dispensed with and there will be no corporations to take from the bench the best legal minds by offering three or four times the federal salary; nor will there be occasion for a Justice of the Supreme Court of Kansas to render a decision that a corporation chartered by Kansas for the sole purpose of building a railway in that State has the right and power, under such charter, to guarantee the bonds of corporations building railways in Old or New Mexico, and shortly after writing such decision be carted all over the seaboard States in one of the luxurious private cars of such corporation. Under national ownership such judges would pay their traveling expenses in the ordinary manner and not half as many judges would travel on passes. There are many judges whose decisions any number of passes would not affect, but if passes are not to have any effect upon legislation and litigation why are congressmen, legislators, judges and other court officials singled out for this kind of martyrdom? If the men who attain these positions remained private citizens would passes be thrust upon them?

Although the reports of the Victorian Commissioners show in detail all the expenditures of railway administration, yet not one dollar is set down for attorneys' salaries or for legal expenses, and it is presumed that the ordinary law officers of the government attend to the little legal business arising, and yet, judging from reports made by Kansas roads, the expenditures of the corporate owned railways of the United States for attorneys and other legal expenses are at least two per cent. of the entire cost of operating the roads, and yearly aggregate some $14,000,000, all of which is taken directly from railway users, and is a direct tax, which would be saved under national ownership, as United States district attorneys could attend to such legal business as might arise. This expenditure is incurred in endless controversies between the corporations; in wrecking railways; in plundering the shareholders; in contending against state and federal regulations; in manipulating elections and legislation, and in wearing out such citizens as seek legal redress for some of the many outrageous acts of oppression practiced by the corporations. Once the government was in control, these lawyers would be relegated to some employment where they would do less harm, even if not engaged in a more honorable vocation than that of trying to defeat justice by the use of such questionable means as the control of the vast revenues of the corporations placed in their hands.

Is it possible that railway companies can legitimately use anything like $14,000,000 yearly in protecting their rights in the courts?

The president of the Union Pacific tells us that : "The courts are open to redress all real grievances of the citizens." There is probably no man in the United States better aware than is Sidney Dillon that no citizen, unless he has as much wealth as the president of the Union Pacific, can successfully contest a case of any importance in the courts with one of these corporations which make a business, as a warning to other possible plaintiffs, of wearing out the unfortunate plaintiff with the laws costly delays; and failing in this do not hesitate to spirit away the plaintiff's witnesses, and to pack and buy juries—retaining a special class of attorneys for this work—the command of great corporate revenues enabling them to accomplish their ends, and to utterly ruin nearly every man having the hardihood to seek Mr. Dillon's lauded legal redress, and when they have accomplished such nefarious object the entire cost is charged back to the public and collected in the form of tolls upon traffic. Laws are utterly powerless to restrain the corporations, and Mr. Dillon tells us how easy it is for them to evade by pleading compliance, when there has been no compliance, and then having the expert servants of the corporation swear there has been.

With the goverment operating the railways every citizen riding would pay fare adding immensely to the revenues. Few have any conception of the proportion who travel free, and half a century's experience renders it doubtful if the pass evil—so much greater than ever was the franking privileges—can be eliminated otherwise than by national ownership. From the experience of the writer as an auditor of railway accounts, and as an executive officer issuing passes, he is able to say that fully ten per cent. travel free, the result being that the great mass of railway users are yearly mulcted some $20,000,000 for the benefit of the favored minority, hence it is evident that if all were required to pay for railway services, as they are for mail services, the rates might be reduced ten per cent. or more, and the corporate revenues be no less, and the operating expenses no more. In no other country—unless it be under the same system in Canada—are nine-tenths of the people taxed to pay the traveling expenses of the other tenth. By what right do the corporations tax the public that members of congress, legislators, judges and other court officials and their families may ride free? Why is it that when a legislature is in session that passes are as plentiful as leaves in the forest in autumn?

The writer, as an executive officer of a railway company having authority to issue passes, has, during a session of the legislature, signed vast numbers of blank passes at the request of the legislative agents of such company and under instructions of the president of the corporation to furnish such lobby agents with all the passes they should ask for.

No reports of passes issued are made either to state or federal governments, or to confiding share-holders, and should such reports be asked for, by state or nation, in order to measure the extent of this evil, the Sidney Dillons would rush into print and tell us it was a piece of impertinence for any citizen (or the public) to enquire into the extent of or the manner in which the corporation dispensed their favors. The only way to kill this monster is to put the instruments of transportation under such control as only national ownership can give. Laws and agreements between the corporations have been proven, time and again, wholly ineffective even to lessen this great and corrupting evil.

In every conceivable way are the net revenues of the corporations depleted and needless burthens imposed upon the public, but one of the worst is the system of paying commissions for the diversion of traffic to particular lines, often the least direct. The more common practice is to pay such commissions to agents of connecting lines where it is possible to send the traffic over any one of two or more routes, and the one which may, by the payment of such commission secure the carrying of the passenger (or merchandise) may be the least desirable, and the one which would never have been taken but for the prevarications of an agent, bribed by a commission to make false representations as to the desirableness of the route he selects for the confiding passenger.

This is but one of many phases of the commission evil, another being that these sums are ultimately paid, not by the corporations, but by the users of the railways, and but for the payment of such commissions the rates might be reduced in like amounts. Aside from commissions paid for diverting passenger traffic great sums are paid for "influencing" and "routing" freight traffic, and these sums, while paid to outsiders, or so-called brokers, are frequently divided with railway officials. When the writer was in charge of the transportation accounts of a railway running east from Chicago, it was a part of his duties to certify to the correctness of the vouchers on which commission payments were made, and he became aware of the fact that one Chicago brokerage firm was being paid a commission of from three to five cents per hundred pounds on nearly all the flour, grain, packing house, and distillery products being shipped out of Chicago over this railway, no matter where such shipment might originate, many of them, in fact, originating on and far west of the Mississippi river, and when he objected to certifying to shipments with which it was clear that the Chicago parties could have had nothing to do, he was told by the manager that his duties ended when he had ascertained and certified that such shipments had been made from Chicago station. From investigations instituted by the writer, he soon learned that some one connected with the management was deeply interested in the payment of the largest sums possible as commission.

The corporations have ineffectually wrestled with the commission evil, and any number of agreements have been entered into to do away with it; but it is so thoroughly entrenched, and so many of their officials have an interest in its perpetuation, that they are utterly powerless in the presence of a system which imposes great and needless burthens upon their patrons, but which will die the day the government takes possession of the railways, as then there will be no corporations ready to pay for the diversion of traffic. National ownership alone can dispose of an administrative evil that, from such data as is obtainable, appears to cost the public from $20,000,000 to $25,000,000 per annum.

Mr. Meany, in his *Sun* article, summarizes six causes for the diminution of railway dividends and remarks: "It is unnecessary to dwell at any great length upon the first five mentioned reasons, but too much could not be said on the sixth. It is now nearly seven years since James McHenry of London (and New York, Pennsylvania and Ohio Railway litigation fame) openly charged railway managers, in an interview published in the *Sun*, with criminal collusion in the matter of securing extraordinary privileges and unapproachable contracts with their several corporations for favored fast freight lines, express routes, bridge companies, etc., etc., in all the benefits of which such managers shared to a very great extent. On that occasion Mr. McHenry was promptly cried down. Would he be cried down to-day?"

As a rule American railways pay the highest salaries in the world for those engaged in directing business operations, but such salaries are not paid because transcendant talents are necessary to conduct the ordinary operations of railway administration, but for the purpose of check-mating the chicanery of corporate competitors. In other words, these exceptionally high salaries are paid for the purpose, and because their recipients are believed to have the ability to hold up their end in unscrupulous corporate warfare where, as one railway president expressed it, "the greatest liar comes out ahead." With the government operating the railways, there would be no conflicting interests necessitating the employment of such costly officials whose diplomatic talents might well be dispensed with, while the running of trains, and the conduct of the real work of operating the roads, could be left to the same officials as, at moderate salaries, now perform such duties, and consolidation of all the conflicting interests in the hands of the government will enable the people to dispense with the services of the high-priced managers now almost exclusively engaged in "keeping even with the other fellow" as well as with the costly staffs assisting such managers in keeping even, and the savings resulting may be estimated at from $4,000,000 to $5,000,000 per year.

Government control will enable railway users to dispense with the services of such high-priced umpires as Mr. Aldace F. Walker, as well as of all other officials of 68 traffic associations, fruitlessly laboring to prevent each of 500 corporations from getting the start of its fellows, and trying to prevent each of the 500 from absorbing an undue share of the traffic. It appears that each of these costly peace-making attachments has an average of seven corporations to watch.

Referring to traffic associations, and their vain endeavors to keep the corporations within sight of commercial ethics the Interstate Commerce Commission says: "But the most important provisions of the law have not so often been directly violated as they have been nullified through devices, carefully framed with legal assistance,—here is one of the places where the high-priced lawyer gets in his work—with a view to this very end, and in the belief that when brought to legal test the device hit upon would not be held by the courts to be so distinctly opposed to the terms of the law as to be criminally punishable." In this connection it is well to remember what Mr. Dillon tells us of the ease with which the laws can be evaded.

With national ownership the expenditures involved in the maintenance of traffic associations would be saved and railway users relieved of a tax that, judging from the reports of a limited number of corporations of their contributions towards the support of such organizations, must annually amount to between four and five million dollars.

Of the six hundred corporations operating railways probably five hundred maintain costly general offices where president, treasurer and secretary spend the time surrounded by an expensive staff. The majority of such offices are off the lines of the respective corporations in the larger cities where high rents are paid and great expenses are entailed that proper attention may be given to the bolstering or depressing the price of the corporation's shares as the management may be long or short of the market. So far as the utility of the railways is concerned, as instruments of anything but speculation, such offices and officers might as well be located in the moon and their cost saved to the public. The average yearly cost of such offices and officers is more than $50,000 and the transfer of the railways to the nation would, in this matter alone, effect an annual saving of more than $25,000,000 as both offices and officials could be dispensed with and the service be no less efficient.

Moreover, with the nation owning the railways, the indirect but no less onerous tax levied upon the industries of the country by the thousands of speculators who make day hideous on the stock exchanges would be abrogated, as then there would be neither railway share or bond for these harpies to make shuttle-cocks of, and this would be another economy due to such ownership.

Railways spend enormous sums in advertising, the most of which national ownership would save, as it would be no more necessary to advertise the advantages of any particular line than it is to advertise the advantages of any given mail route. From reports made by railway corporations to some of the Western States, it appears that something over one per cent. of operating expenses are absorbed in advertising, aggregating something like $7,000,000 per year, of which we may assume that but $5,000,000 would be saved, as it would be still desirable to advertise train departures and arrivals.

A still greater expense is involved in the maintenance of freight and passenger offices off the respective lines, for the purpose of securing a portion of the competitive traffic. In this way vast sums are expended in the payment of rents and as salaries of hordes of agents, solicitors, clerks, etc., etc. Taking the known expenditures for this purpose of a given mileage, it is estimated that the aggregate is not less than $15,000,000 yearly, all of which is a tax upon the public that would be saved did the government operate the railways.

Under government control discriminations against localities would cease, whereas now localities are discriminated against because managers are interested in real estate elsewhere or are interested in diverting traffic in certain directions. Again, under corporate management, it is for the interest of the company to haul a commodity as far as possible over its own lines (with the government owning all the lines this motive will lose its force) and thus traffic is forced into unnatural channels. For instance, much of the grain from Kansas should find its way to foreign markets via the short route to the Gulf, the distance to tide water by this route being less than half what it is to the Atlantic; yet so opposed to this natural route are the interests of the majority of the corporations controlling the traffic associations which now dictate to the people what routes their traffic shall take, that the rates to the Gulf are kept so high as to force the traffic to the lakes and to the Atlantic, and as all the railways leading to the Gulf have lines running eastward, the much lauded corporate competition fails to help out the citizens of Kansas, who are subjected to the domination of the new tyrant denominated a "Traffic Association." With the nation operating the railways all this would be changed and localities favorably located would be able to reap the benefits which such location should give, and should such a condition ever obtain the farmers of Western Iowa will not then ship corn to the drouth-stricken portion of Kansas for fifteen cents per one hundred pounds while the Kansas corn-grower, living within seventy-five miles of the same market, is charged ten cents per one hundred pounds for a haul one-eighth as long. By such rates the railways force the hauling of corn from Iowa to Western Kansas, and then force the corn-grower of Central Kansas to send his corn eastward, the result being two long hauls where one short one would suffice, but then the corporations would have absorbed less of the substance of the people.

Another and incalculable benefit which would result from national ownership would be the relief of state and national legislation from the pressure and corrupting practices of railway corporations, which constitute one of the greatest dangers to which republican institutions can be subjected. This alone renders the nationalization of the railways most desirable, and at the same time such nationalization would have the effect of emancipating a large part of the press from a galling thraldom to the corporations.

With the nation operating the railways we may have some hope that rates will be reduced by some system resembling the Hungarian zone, which has had the effect of reducing local passenger rates about forty per cent., resulting in such an increase of traffic as to greatly increase the revenues of the roads, the average of rates by ordinary third-class trains being about three-fourths of a cent per mile, and one and a half cents per mile for first-class express trains.

In Victoria the parcel or express business is done by the government railways, and the rates are not one-half what they are with us when farmed out to a second lot of corporations. Space does not permit the discussion or even the statement of the many salutary phases of government control as developed in the various countries of Europe, and it is not necessary as there are abundant reasons to be found in conditions existing at home for making the proposed change.

By far the most menacing feature of continued corporate ownership is the power over the money markets, which it places in the hands of unscrupulous men, any half dozen of whom can, at such a time as that following the failure of the Barings, destroy the welfare of millions and plunge the country into all the horrors of a money panic. Whether it be true or not there are many who believe that a small coterie who had information before the public of the condition of Baring Brothers, and that a block of many millions of railway securities, held by that house, were being (or soon would be) pressed upon the market, entered into a conspiracy for the purpose of locking up money, and thereby depressing prices in order to secure, at low cost, the control of certain coveted railways. The railways were secured, and there is not much doubt that they had been lying in wait for such a critical condition of the money markets to accomplish this purpose, which still further enhances their power for evil. With the railways nationalized not only would there be no temptation for such nefarious operations but the power of such men over values would be greatly lessened if not wholly destroyed as there would be no railway shares for them to play fast and loose with and as money, instead of being tied up in loans on chromos representing little but water would seek investment in bona-fide enterprises their operations would have little influence and would certainly have no such baleful power over the industries of the country as their ability to affect the value of railway shares—on which such immense sums are now loaned on call—gives them they being able, by locking up a few millions when the money-market is in the condition which obtained at the time of the Baring collapse, to force the calling of loans and the slaughtering of vast numbers of shares carrying the control of the railways they covet. If only for the purpose of divesting "the dangerous wealthy classes" of this frightful power, national ownership would be worth many times its cost, and without such ownership a score of manipulators are soon likely to be complete masters of the republic and all its industrial interests; hence the question reverts to the form stated in the opening of this paper: Shall the nation accept as a master a political party that may be dislodged by the use of the ballot or shall the republic be dominated by a master in the form of a score of unscrupulous Goulds, Vanderbilts and Huntingtons who cannot be dislodged and who never die?

Assuming that $30,000 per mile is the maximum cost of existing railways—as is shown in *"The Arena"* for February—and that there are 160,000 miles, it would give a total valuation of $4,800,000,000, but that there may be no complaint that the nation is dealing unfairly with the owners of much water, it will be well to add 25 per cent. to what will be found to be the outside value of the railways when condemned under the law of eminent domain, and assuming that $6,000,000,000 of three per ceut. bonds are issued in order to make payment therefor, and it involves an interest charge of $180,000,000, to which add $670,000,000, as the cost of maintenance and operation, and $50,000,000 us a sinking fund, and we have a total annual cost for railway service, of $900,000,000 as against a present cost of $1,050,000,000 ($950,000,000 from traffic earnings, and $85,000,000 from other sources of railway revenue), resulting in a net annual saving to the public of $150,000,000, to which must be added the various savings which it has been estimated would result from government control, and which, for the convenience of the reader, are here recapitulated, namely:

Saving from consolidation of depots and staffs	$ 20,000,000
Saving from exclusive use of shortest routes	25,000,000
Saving in attorneys' salaries and legal expenses	12,000,000
Saving from the abrogation of the pass evil	30,000,000
Saving from the abrogation of the commission system	20,000,000
Saving by dispensing with high priced managers and staffs	4,000,000
Saving by disbanding traffic associations	4,000,000
Saving by dispensing with presidents, etc	25,000,000
Saving by abolishing (all but local) offices, solicitors, etc	15,000,000
Saving of five-sevenths of the advertising account	5,000,000
Total savings by reason of better administration	$160,000,000

It would appear that after yearly setting aside $50,000,000 as a sinking fund, that there are the best of reasons for believing that the cost of the railway service would be $310,000,000 less than under corporate management.

That $6,000,000,000 is much more than it would cost to duplicate existing railways, will not be questioned by the disinterested familiar with late reductions in the cost of construction, and that such a valuation is excessive is manifest from the fact that it is much more than the market value of all the railway bonds and shares in existence.

Mr. John P. Meany, in the *Railway Review* of February 7th, 1891, says: "It is safe to assume that the market valuation of the entire $4,500,000,000 of railroad stock in existence would not average more than $30 per share, or say $1,350,000,000 in all." And in his *Sun* article he states that fully $500,000,000 of this stock is duplicated, so that the "live" capital stock outstanding is really but $4,000,000,000, which, at $30 per share, would have an aggregate value of $1,200,000,000. Mr. Meany states that there are also duplications of bond issues amounting to some $300,000,000, leaving the live outstanding bonds at $4,500,000,000, and many corporations failing to pay interest, some issues are selling as low as 12 per cent. of par, making it safe to call the average market value of bonds 90 per cent. of their face value, and their aggregate value $4,050,000,000, to which add value of "live" capital stock, $1,200,000,000, and the total market value of bonds and stock is $5,250,000,000, being at the rate of $32,800 per mile for the 160,000 miles in operation.

After many years of familiarity with the turgid and obscure statements issued by American railway corporations, and which are usually of such a character that the more they are studied the less the shareholder knows of the affairs of the corporation, it is very refreshing to read the report of the Railway Commissioners of any one of the Australian colonies, where every item of expenditure is made clear, and where words are not used for the purpose of misleading.

The last Victorian report shows this new and sparsely settled country as able to borrow money, with which to build national railways, at 3½ per cent. per annum. How many American corporations are able to borrow money at such a rate? This saving in the interest charge directly benefits the public, and is due to national ownership, and a like saving will be made by the nationalization of American railways.

This report also shows that while the country is so rugged that in many cases the gradients are as great as 130 feet per mile, and the cost of labor and supplies more than here, the roads are operated at less cost, as measured by the expense per train mile, than in the favored regions of the United States. The Kansas City, Fort Scott and Memphis Railway is, admittedly, one of the best managed and most economically operated railways in the West, and with an abundance of very cheap coal,* low gradients and running more trains than do the Victorian railways, should be operated much more cheaply, yet the cost of operating this road, as measured by the cost per train mile,—and this is the best possible criterion of economy in operation—is one-third greater than on the government owned railways of Victoria.

An excellent measure of the efficiency of the management is the number of casualties, as proportioned to the number of passengers carried and men employed, which is very great in such countries as Russia, Roumania and Portugal; but in Victoria and other Australian colonies, the proportion is far less than in the United States, more attention being given to the adoption of such safety devices as interlocking switches, etc., and all the stations and crossings are provided with gates and otherwise better guarded than with us where the corporations are much more intent upon paying dividends than in serving the public, or in saving life and limb, while on the government operated railways of Victoria, the management devotes its attention—with due regard to economy—to the convenience, comfort and safety of railway users, and employes, having no bond or shareholders to provide for.

In the United States one of the useless traffic associations pays its chief umpire nearly as much as Victoria pays its entire commission.

Those desirous of entering the railway service of Victoria are subjected to such rigid examination as to qualifications and character, that but little more than one-third are able to pass the ordeal, and a high standard of excellence in the personnel of the service results, and when these servants are disabled, or worn out by long service, they are pensioned or given a retiring allowance, and this system tends to reduce the inclination to strike, as a man who has been years in the service will long hesitate before he forfeits his right to a provision of this kind.

All the Australian reports and accounts, which have come under the observation of the writer, are models of conciseness and clearness and show that there is nothing inherent in railway accounts rendering it necessary that they be made obscure and misleading.

Neither in the Australian reports nor in the Colonial press is there the least evidence of discriminations against individuals or localities, and this one fact is an argument of greater force in favor of national ownership than all that have ever been advanced against it.

*Coal on the line named is worth about $1.50 per ton at the mines, while inferior coal is worth $3.75 per ton at the mines in Victoria.

THE ECONOMIST'S OPINION OF MARKET WRECKING.

The claim is persistently made, by the opponents of the Butterworth bill, that short-selling can in no wise injure the producer of cotton, grain and other staple products, but on the other hand is a great and inestimable benefit to the producer, and that the agitation of the subject is carried on by demagogues for the purpose of irritating the farmer and leading him to place himself in opposition to the very men who, by their short-selling, create a market for his products and enable him to secure a better price. Without asking if the practice of short-selling can possibly increase the number of consumers or the per capita consumption, a sufficient answer to all that has ever been advanced in favor of short-selling is to be found in the June 20th issue of so pronounced an organ of Chicago interests as the Chicago *Economist*, where it is said, editorially, that:

"This is the season when farmers begin to grumble against Boards of Trade, and assert that short-sellers are engaged in their usual effort to make a low market for farm products. There is some ground for their irritation. It is possible that the system of trading in futures, now so popular, has been carried to an abuse. * * * * It is within the range of possibility that the Exchanges may be brought to see that after all a change in the system of trading may not operate to their disadvantage. It may be found possible to trade in grain (and cotton) on a cash basis, as stocks are traded in on the New York Exchange. No pretense is made that the volume of speculation is curtailed to any important extent in stocks, by reason of the fact that all transactions are strictly for cash * * * * The seller of stocks may not have the stocks to deliver at the time he makes the trade, but he must, in some manner, procure them. * * * * If he does not already own them, he does this by borrowing the stocks and paying therefor a small percentage, which percentage is regulated by the urgency of the demand from short-sellers. Why could not this plan be put in force in regard to grain, (cotton, etc.)? Would not such a system *result in equalizing the carrying charges, which are a serious handicap upon investors and upon the property itself?*

Under existing conditions grain and cotton is burthened with a tax from the moment the seed is put in the ground. This tax does not begin to accumulate, apparently, until the grain has left the harvest field and is on the way to the great markets. But as a matter of fact, the property is handicaped from its inception.

Investors and *producers* have the burthen to carry, and the short-sellers have the advantage to the extent of the full accumulation of charges of all sorts—transportation, storage, insurance, commissions, etc. *They* (the short-sellers) *figure that the property cannot carry this burthen and advance to a point beyond it which will give the holders of the* (real) *property a profit.*

They argue generally that grain (and cotton) will not be worth any more one, two or six months hence than now, and that they have just the advantage over investors and producers which is represented by all these accumulated charges (as they invest nothing in the sort of stuff in which they deal) hence they feel a certain degree of safety in offering property (promises) for future delivery at prices which pays them a liberal premium, *thereby gaining all these carrying charges just as surely as if they owned the elevators in which the grain was stored, the railroads upon which it was carried and the insurance companies and banks which collect additional tolls.*

If the short-sellers were compelled to deliver the grain they sell and pay the owner a per cent. for the property to deliver on contracts the carrying charges would be fairly equalized in the long run.

Possibly, also, this process might result in filling the warehouses with grain, for capital will find profitable employment in investments in large quantities of grain as a basis for such operations. (And this would, at such seasons as when more grain was being marketed than was required for immediate consumption, relieve the market of undue pressure).

"Excessive short-selling (all short-selling is excessive) *which is beyond any question a burthen upon production, and a serious handicap upon investment of* * * * *capital* would be measurably reduced * * * and the onerous feature would be measurably eliminated. (If it is a wrong why not eliminate it wholly).

"A little experience might relieve the speculative trade of the horror which it now feels of contact with the actual grain. * * * * A system of cash dealings would certainly give the producer an even chance with the short-seller, which he does not now enjoy."

"The strangulation of the Butterworth bill last winter merely postponed action; it did not kill the sentiment that was back of it, or remove the grievance."

C. A. PILLSBURY'S OPINION OF MARKET WRECKING.

The utterances of an organ of Chicago interests, in the best sense of the term, may well be supplemented by the opinion of one who is, beyond a doubt, the greatest dealer in the world in the products of the soil, and one who yearly grinds more than half as much actual wheat into flour as reaches the Chicago markets.

The following excerpts are made from an interview with Mr. C. A. Pillsbury, published in the Minneapolis *Daily Market Record :*

" While talking with respect to the matter of limitation of wheat production, so that for the last three years there has been a decrease of the reserves, Mr. C. A. Pillsbury. the miller, says: ' If the world was entirely out of wheat at the end of this crop, and our crop was only eleven months' supply, under the old method of doing business wheat would sell at from $1.50 to $2 per bushel, but under the new method the heavy short-seller in Chicago would sell 10,000,000 or 15,000,000 bushels out while he was talking higher markets, and then on some weak spot sell two or three millions more when there was no demand for it, in order to break the markets down to 60 or 70 cents a bushel, then buy in his short sales, and this would discourage all holders of wheat, until the scarcity was actually felt and there was hardly anyone holding any wheat to get the benefit of the advance.

"Mr. C. Wood Davis, in a recent elaborate article in the "Arena" gave his conclusions that the consumption of wheat throughout the world had already overtaken production, and at so early a date as 1896 the United States will have ceased to export wheat."

"In reference to Mr. Davis' idea Mr. Pillsbury said: *I think Mr Davis' theory is right, but it will not do any one much good, no matter how short the crops are, until short-selling of wheat by those who do not own a bushel can be stopped.* As I said before, farmers may talk about railroad and elevator charges, but if the elevators handled their wheat for nothing and railroads hauled it without compensation, these benefits would not begin to offset the injuries which they receive from the Board of Trade."

"My opinion is that *we have been eating up the wheat reserve during the last five years and that at the end of the last crop the visible (supply) all over the world was about as low as practicable on even the new method of doing business and carrying stock, and I shall be surprised if before a new crop is fit to use, we do not see a worse situation.*"

"As long, however, as this short selling is not circumscribed by the strong arm of the law these advances in wheat will only come at the latter end of the crop year when farmers have sold nearly all their grain, and when neither the farmers nor the mercantile communities nor the business men in the State will get the benefit of the fact that the world is not producing as much bread-stuff as it is consuming."

THE MARKET WRECKER PREVENTS AN ADVANCE IN VALUES.

Not only is the world short of food by reason of a deficient cultivated acreage, but the disaster which has befallen the crops of Europe renders it certain that the last of the reserves will disappear and the grain harvested in 1892 go into empty granaries, and that the supplies for the 1892-3 cereal year will be trenched upon by enormous drafts made upon India, South America and Australasia, early in 1892, for the purpose of feeding the famishing people of Europe and this exhaustion of all reserves; the trenching upon future supplies and the well established deficient acreage would assure high prices for a long term of years but for short selling upon the Boards of Trade, such practices constituting an evil of great magnitude as well as a great menace to the prosperity of the farmer, and, by lessening his purchasing power, a like menace to the prosperity of all employed in production or distribution.

So long as the market wrecking option dealer, without owning or controlling a pound of the products that he offers to sell in limitless quantities, can determine prices by placing his fictitious products in competition with the products of the farm, just so long will the farmer be uncertain of a reward for the labor and capital employed, and just so long will short periods of great commercial activity be followed by prolonged ones of stagnation.

The immoral practices of the short-seller have yearly deprived the farmer of from ten to twenty-five per cent. of the price he otherwise would have obtained for his products, and in this way his purchasing power has been greatly lessened, resulting in equal loss to the artisan, laborer, manufacturer, merchant and transporter, and a like loss is menaced so long as the short-selling market wrecker is permitted to pursue the nefarious calling of placing his fictions in competition with the products of the farm.

It requires land upon which to grow real products, and in the United States there is employed in the production of food, fiber and forage 700,000,000 acres, or more, and every pound of the products of the soil which the farmer offers represents the expenditure of a definite amount of money and labor, and the volume of product which he can offer is limited by the amount of land in cultivation, its fertility and meteorological conditions which last render the result sufficiently uncertain without the baleful work of the short-seller. On the other hand the short-selling market wrecker neither owns nor needs land; he expends no money in producing what he offers; neither does he toil; his crop is subject to no climatic contingencies; is harvested without labor, and the amount offered is limited only by his assurance and lung power, both of which are phenomenal, *and yet it is these limitless offers of fictions which have cost neither money nor effort*—and not what the farmer has produced at the cost of such infinite care and labor—which determines the price which the farmer shall receive for the products of his land and toil. Thus does the market wrecker reap where he has not sown. Thus does this worthless drone despoil the industrious farmer of a just reward for his labor.

How much longer shall the farmer's products, grown at an enormous expenditure of capital and labor, be forced to compete with the limitless and *costless* products of the lungs of the short-seller?

Is there another business that is subjected to such unfair and immoral competition?

Would other than farmers submit to such gross injustice when they have the power to control legislation and could, by the enactment of laws taxing the "Board-of-Trade-Gambler" out of existence, secure the reward due for their labors and yet fail to do so while their products are forced to compete with the imaginary products of a horde of parasites and harpies?

Are not the harpies of the "Board of Trade" as much worse than the managers of a "bunco or skin game" as the stealing of hundreds of millions a year *from those who take no part in the game* is worse than the taking a few dollars from some fellow who voluntarily goes into a skin game thinking he has a sure thing of turning up the right card and thus beating the dealer? In the market-wrecking game the farmer is not even given a chance, by the three-card sharps of the Board-of-Trade, to see the cards that rob him of the reward for his labor.

For years the market-wreckers have been able, by the short-selling device, to deprive the farmer of a due reward and notwithstanding the deficient—world's—acreage they will remain a grave menace to his prosperity, and that of the country, so long as permitted to pursue their nefarious calling of selling the crops before they are grown; of selling the property of the farmer, without his consent, and thereby fixing a price for property in which they have no legitimate interest.

Although existing abnormal conditions may enable the farmer—despite the baleful work of the short-seller—to get more than usual for this year's crop of grain, even if much less than what they should receive, yet the wreckers have taken and are likely to retain complete control of the cotton market until they have forced the cotton grower to the condition in which they had placed the grain grower until short crops enabled the market to get partially from under their control, but let there be but the promise of fair grain crops next summer and the wrecker will resume entire control of the markets and prices be again hammered down to an unremunerative level and the process of depressing prices below a natural level continue until the market-wrecker shall have been taxed out of existence.

SOME PHASES OF SHORT SELLING.

The short-seller produces nothing; he performs no service, and is but a destroyer of the value of other men's property.

The legitimate trader, be he a buyer either for immediate consumption or to hold for an advance, takes the product off the market thereby steadying demand and enabling the producer to secure a fair price for his property.

The short-seller needs little or no capital to enable him to wreck values as is made clear by the failures of Dunham & Co. and Pardridge. Dunham, with a capital of but $25,000, was carrying a line of shorts aggregating 10,000,000 bushels; equal to but two and a half cents per bushel, and this flat grain, representing such an insignificant sum in forfeits put up to assure the other gambler that Dunham would not go back on the game, came in direct competition with and depressed the price (just as effectually as though it were real grain) of that grown by the farmer at the cost of much expenditure of capital and infinite labor. Could anything be more unfair?

When, by the sudden advance of wheat in August, the great bear (Pardridge) was forced into liquidation at a reported loss of $1,000,000, he must have had out a short line of at least 20,000,000 bushels, as the advance was but 5 cents, and as he had been repeatedly called for margins during the advance, it would appear that the actual investment in these enormous short sales—equal to nearly one-twentieth of an average crop—could not have exceeded two cents a bushel and yet this man has, repeatedly, with such relatively infinitesimal investments, been able to depress the price of all the grain owned by millions of farmers and deprive them of the reward due for their labors.

In a published interview he is reported to have said that: "Had not my money given out I could and would have sent the price of wheat to 75 cents; what I lost was only velvet (profits) from my operations since April."

In the four months required to secure profits reported to be $1,000,000, what were the losses of American farmers consequent upon the operations of these short-selling gamblers?

Can there be a reasonable doubt that in consequence of short-selling the producer is forced to accept from ten to twenty-five per cent. less for his cotton and grain than he ought to and otherwise would receive?

If Board of Trade men must gamble why not bet on a game of poker or faro, or upon a horse race? In such case only the participants, or possibly their employers from whom has been stolen the money wagered, would suffer injury.

Short-selling enables the European to throw immense quantities of fictitious products upon our markets thereby depressing the price when he takes in the cash product at the price he has established by such nefarious practices. Moreover, when he has bought a cargo of Indian or Russian wheat he sells an equal quantity short in our market, and thus forces the American farmer, by the short-selling device, to become his insurer and, this too, without paying him a cent of premium. By the short-selling device the American farmer is made to assume all the risks attendant upon European importation of wheat bought from his competitors in India and Russia.

By selling the growing crop short the market wrecker is continually proclaiming that it will be so great as to swamp the markets of the world, and by persistently pursuing this course he is often able to make both producer and consumer believe that such is the case.

Prices are never as low as the market-wrecker says they should be, and the lower they get, with profits in hand, the harder they pound them with limitless offers.

In selling short a product which has cost neither money nor effort, the market-wrecker requires little besides audacity, lung power and an imagination which can evoke enormous crops and commercial disaster at will. Such is his entire capital and stock in trade, and yet so enormous is the volume of these transactions in fictions that immense sums—in the aggregate—are constantly tied up in margins; sums probably several times as great as would be required to handle all the actual grain seeking a market, and in this way is a needless tax levied upon the industries of the country and a fictitious scarcity of money brought about, such scarcity tending, at all times, to still further depress prices for real products.

The reductions in the price of products which the operations of the market-wrecker effect are doubtless such as to absorb a very large proportion of the ordinary profits of production thus greatly lessening the purchasing power of the farmer and this, by reaction, directly affects the prosperity of all employed in distribution, or other forms of production, hence the entire community suffers from the evil of short-selling.

When wheat is selling at $1 the short-seller goes upon the market and offers it for delivery one to six months in the future for 95 cents, and can only secure a profit by breaking the price, and in order to do this resorts to the fabrication of such falsehoods as his experience leads him to believe will effect the end desired. He relies upon such fabrications, not the offering of actual products, to reduce the price to a level that will permit his winning the wager.

Frequently the big bears cry the market down by persistent offerings of immense quantities while their brokers, upon the other side of the pit, are taking all that themselves and other parties offer, so that even should the market happen to advance they cannot lose while they are thus enabled to cover outstanding short sales at a profit on that bought from others at the price they have established by their "wash sales," as is shown in the following telegrams from a broker to his principal at Kansas City:

"CHICAGO, June 4th, 1891.—J. S. & Co., Kansas City: Ribs ninety, lard twenty-five, pork fifty, easy. Bears hammering but buying through brokers.   ROBERTS."

From and to same parties on the same day:

"Market steady now; bears doing everything to break market; weakness of corn helping them.   ROBERTS."

Destroy the profits of short-selling by placing a sufficient tax upon every such transaction and every incentive to force a decline would disappear, and when such incentive disappears prices will be affected only by the volume of real products offering, and supply and demand will once more determine in which direction values shall move, and every dealer being an owner will have a direct interest in sustaining prices, whereas the great majority of the so-called dealers are now interested in depressing prices, as their entire profits are derived from short-selling.

All Board of Trade speculators derive their support from the unjust tolls which short-selling enables them to levy upon the farmer and as they are, like other gamblers, reckless spendthrifts and most extravagant livers and number, with their affiliated hordes, at least 20,000; and assuming that their annual expenditures are no more than $5,000 each, it follows that these worse than useless parasites yearly mulct the farmers of the country in the sum of $100,000,000. What is worse than this they act as a maguet that draws many of the brightest youths into this whirlpool, and most of the embezzlements of bank presidents cashiers, clerks and tellers, as well as those of the employes of commercial houses, are due and directly traceable to the craze for speculative gambling that has its birthplace and habitat upon the Board of Trade.

Add but ten per cent. to the value of the products of the farm by destroying short-selling and the farmer would not only be able to pay his debts, but those of the Nation, State and Municipality.

Was it impossible to wreck values by short-selling prices would be far more steady and monied men would be willing to buy actual products for investment, but now so frequent, erratic and rapid are the fluctuations in values, consequent upon the continual effort of the short-seller to put down prices, that the merchant is deterred from investing in property the price of which is determined by such abnormal methods.

It has long been axiomatic that property that is hawked from one to another in search of a buyer becomes stale and practically unsalable at anything near its real value, and this is just what the short-seller and non-owner is constantly doing with property of the farmer *without the owner's consent* and against his most earnest protest. The result is that which always follows when property is thus hawked about in search of a buyer. There is but one remedy possible, and that is for Congress to exercise the taxing power for the protection of the five millions of cotton and grain growers and tax the 20,000 market-wrecking short-selling gamblers of the Boards of Trade out of existence, and thus relieve production of an intolerable burthen.

The market wrecker has erected a toll bridge on the highway of commerce where there is no stream to cross.

Should not farmers, in and out of season, write and talk to their senators and representatives in Congress persistently until the Butterworth bill, or even a more effective measure, becomes a law?

Why should not the farmer make life a burthen to the law maker until he grants the required protection to the greatest industry of the nation?

Shall all other interests be "protected" and only the farmer be left without the sadly needed protection while he alone is taxed for the benefit of the ' protected classes?''

OPINIONS, PROFESSIONAL AND OTHER, OF MARKET WRECKING.

The great short-seller (Pardridge) is reported to have said to the reporter of a Chicago paper that had his money not have run short—he was unable to create fiat money as readily as he could flat grain—he could and would have forced the price of wheat to 75 cents, and one of his brokers said that if wheat was selling at 5 cents per bushel he would be unhappy if he could not force it to four and a half.

Leopold Bloom, who made a million or more by gambling on the Board and is reported to have lost $35,000 in a "brace" game of faro with two other Board of Trade operators (and which he refused to pay), hence is competent to express an opinion of Board of Trade as well as other varieties of gambling, says that:

"It is too much of a strain on a man. One is under pressure all the time. He is betting his money against the market. If he buys and she goes up he wins, but if she goes down he is a loser. *Its a plain game of gamble, but it's legal and faro isn't. If they would take the limit off faro it would be a better game than wheat, because you could get quicker action; but with the limit on there isn't money enough in it.* A fellow who is playing against the market (against legitimate supply and demand) takes a good many chances, and now that I've got enough to keep me comfortably I want to rest."

May 28th, 1891, the Board of Trade firm of Kennett & Hopkins is reported to have said:

"From a statistical standpoint the position of wheat has not been stronger for many years, but the huge *offerings* by the bears breaks down the price in the face of the strongest conditions. This may go on for weeks notwithstanding the grain moves eastward in a great flood and is exported as soon as it reaches tide water."

Observed Robert Lindbloom:

"It is hard to buck against the millions of wind wheat that we have to contend with in the wheat pit. The bears are determined that the legitimate news shall produce no effect. We point to the large clearances; they say bah! that is mostly flour; we note the large sales of wheat at St. Louis for export, and they cry, O! that is only Oregon wheat; we bear of the clearance of 700,000 bushels during the last two days from the principal Atlantic ports and t ey go into the pit and sell 20,000,000 bushels of wi.d; meanwhile a great deal of money is made through these deals, and the question arises if it is not the farmer who contributes it?"

Under the date ot May 13th, 1891, a great B ard of Trade house writes:

"There has been tremendous selling of wheat lately upon June scenery. June is still weeks off but the scenery is here all the same, and the almanac players are discounting their theory by taking an early start. The mob is now jumping on wheat and everlastingly whooping it up on that side. It has again become a sure thing to sell wheat short."

When speaking of the efforts of the Chicago Board of Trade to suppress the bucket shops, Mr. C. A. Pillsbury, the great Minneapolis miller, is reported as saying:

'A step which would cure the whole trouble would be to stop the selling of grain for future delivery except by parties who absolutely own or control the product, and would be able to deliver it if called upon. I believe this will be done within a few years, even if the constitution of the United States has to be amended in order to do it.

"It is a perfect mystery to me that the Farmers' Alliances are paying attention to minor evils and overlooking this vampire which is sucking their very life blood.

"The legitimate situation has been such during the last three or four years that wheat should have sold at one dollar per bushel at any railroad station in Minnesota. This tremendous short-selling of hundreds of millions of bushels, which the party selling does not own nor ever expect to own, has knocked the bottom out of the market, as these wind *offerings* and sales have just as much effect upon the market as genuine transactions, and the big bears have been so successful and made such enormous profits from their short sales that they now have an immense following, and the evil has assumed tremendous proportions.

"Production throughout the world, as a whole, has not increased during the last five, and possibly ten years, yet if this short-selling is not stopped there will be no advance in price, despite this fact, except in case of grave disaster to the crops over wide areas.

"The Chicago Board of Trade is now moving in the right direction, but after closing the bucket shops let them close the gambling on their own Board and confine their business to legitimate transactions. When this is done the whole western country would see such prosperity as has not been known for many years. The legitimate conditions are all right for it, but the illegitimate conditions could not be worse."

Mr. Hugh McLennan, one of the earliest traders in grain in Chicago, writes:

"The baker and miller in Europe who in former days had to consider supplies for coming months, is now quieted with his daily cable from Chicago that May wheat is off one cent. Wheat in Chicago is now selling five cents below the average price for last October, while the price in Liverpool is about the same as then. The English markets have held up in spite of the depressing influences exerted from this side of the Atlantic."

"Commission Merchant," in a a communication to the Chicago *Tribune*, writes:

"Every one engaged in the actual handling of grain is asking the cause of the low prices, and many are beginning to recognize the fact that the practice of short-selling has much to do with it, and especially the recent custom of selling immense lines of (short) grain for delivery five or six months from the date of sale."

In the *Tribune* market report for January 13th, it is said that:

"With every encouragement for an advance in prices and a bullish interpretation of the government report to aid them, the local produce markets, after a brief flurry at the opening, declined materially and closed at the lowest point of the day. The depression was due to the raiding of the heavy shorts, who knew their only salvation lay in a successful raid."

In characterizing the stock gamblers of Wall street, the Chicago *Tribune* used the following language, only it is here paraphrased and applied to the Board of Trade market wreckers, to whom it is even more clearly applicable than to those of the Stock Exchange:

"The scum of the United States is gathered upon the Boards of Trade to speculate in the necessaries of life. There is no honesty in the business. Part of it is the outworking of cool calculation to rob by hoodwinking the public, inducing men to sell when they ought to buy if they did anything. The rest is blind chance, a simple betting on the course of prices, and a great deal of it is nothing but the buying and selling of "privileges" which entitles the one party to call for or deliver a quantity of the stuff pretended to be dealt in at a named price if he chooses to do so within some specified time.

"But for the operation of the gamblers these alleged products would not be dealt in. What possible difference can it make to the welfare of the country whether the gamblers continue to exist or not? If they were all to be cleaned out (a la Pardridge) the people would not only be no worse off, but actually vastly better."

The St. Louis *Republic* of August 20th, 1891, says editorially:

"When 11,000,000 bushels of wheat are sold in one day on one Merchants' Exchange, how long will it take to handle the whole crop? And that being first found, how long will it take to handle a poker deck so as to regulate the wheat supply *and establish its price?*

Aside from the disastrous effects of these gambling practices upon the producer, who is an innocent and involuntary victim, they are equally disastrous to the gambler, whom they rob of all right feeling.

Speaking of gambling in all its forms, an eminent English authority says:

"Gambling not only leads to financial ruin, but it produces the most heartless forms of selfishness, and is especially fatal to delicacy and magnanimity of character. It is a peculiarly mean and sordid vice."

Herbert Spencer, in his Study of Sociology, presents two aspects of the immorality of gambling when he says:

"It is gain without merit; and secondly, it is gain through another's loss. Whenever the seller and the buyer are not mutually benefitted the transaction is immoral and rotten and involves dishonesty and deceit on one side or the other."

Some of the moral aspects of gambling in farm products, and the incalculable wrong it works the producer, is well set forth in a recent issue of the (Iowa) *Homestead*. Says the *Homestead:*

"For owners of wheat to sell when at any given period they think the market price is as good as it is going to be is one thing; for men who own no wheat, and mean to own none, to sell for future delivery, is another and very different thing. It is neither more nor less, in substance, than a bet as to what the price will be at the date when, nominally, the delivery is to be made. It is 'backing the judgment' just as much as though a stake were set on the turn of a card. * * * * This backing of judgment, however, is the simplest and least harmful form of grain gambling. The transactions of professional grain gamblers compare with this form about as a sold race, a brace game of faro or Sir William Gordon-Cummings' dealings in baccarat compare with square games, where risks are honestly taken and chance or legitimate skill is permitted to determine them. The professionals, when a deal is decided upon, jump upon the market and sell millions of bushels when they don't own a kernel; they follow the price down with lower and still lower sales, using all kinds of false rumors—as to crops, failures of bankers, and other conditions affecting products and money—as clubs to beat down prices, and at length, when prices have reached the lowest possible notch, they turn in and 'cover their shorts' at the low figure, reaping as stakes the difference between the higher figures at which they have sold and the lower ones at which they have covered their 'short' sales. The means employed to produce the depression, in point of honesty, is not a whit superior to the cheating tricks of the professional card sharp.

"But this falls far short of a full statement of the moral evil involved in grain gambling. When a hundred excited men jump into a Chicago grain pit and play a game, *the result of which, when telegraphed over the country, reduces the value of the contents of every producer's bin five to ten cents a bushel*, the tendency of it all is to confuse the ideas of right and wrong of every man upon whom loss has thus been inflicted.

"As an abstract proposition, every man will admit that demand and supply should regulate price; yet the producers of the country have become so habituated to seeing the law of demand and supply nullified to their injury by gambling manipulations that a very large proportion of them would not hesitate to combine in the creation of an artificial scarcity if they saw their way clear to the accomplishment of such a result. If there had never have been any cotton gambling there would never have been a sub-treasury scheme. if there were no grain gambling there would have been no attempt at a 'farmers' wheat corner.'

"Gambling in farm products has caused such wide-spread injury to persons not in any manner engaged in it, that it is in large measure responsible for some confusion of ideas as to the proposition to fight the devil with fire.

"The entire civilized world has lately been convulsed over the spectacle of a royal game of baccarat at which there was said to have been some cheating, yet the evil of it was confined to the persons engaged in the game. Possibly there are states in the Union which do not make gambling a punishable offense; yet here again, the evil extends no farther than to those who participate it it, or at most to their families. A number of states have quite recently passed laws against pool selling; a species of gambling that is bad enough to merit prohibition, and yet infinitesimally trifling when compared with the millions that are lost and won in grain (and cotton) gambling. Why should the law punish those who play faro and wink at 'futures?' Why forbid poker and permit 'puts and calls?' The former injures in purse and in morals perhaps, only the persons engaged in it; the latter does as much, and besides injures the farmer morally and materially although he be a thousand miles away; materially, for it makes him pay heavy losses on a game in which he does not participate; morally, for it tends to undermine his patriotic regard for a government that permits such injury to be inflicted upon him, and drives him to adopt questionable methods of self protection.

"Organized society has neither soul or future; it must take its punishment as it goes along. The sin of omission which permits a gigantic scheme of gambling under pretense of commerce, involving in its evil effects the innocent with the guilty, will not escape retribution.

"Congress recently adopted measures designed to prevent, to the extent of congressional authority, the business of the Louisiana lottery and the moral sense of the entire community sustained it in the act.

"Lotteries are wrong and demoralizing, and yet they injure only those who voluntarily become their victims. Board of Trade gambling, on the contrary, while equally wrong and demoralizing to the participants does immense injury to vast numbers of people who have nothing whatever to do with it. As long as this form of gambling—which is as bad morally as the worst—is permitted we can hardly escape the conviction of having strained at the lottery gnat and swallowed the Board of Trade camel. Can the nation afford further responsibility for a monster gambling scheme which inflicts great loss upon so large a number of its most industrious and worthy citizens, even when they take no voluntary part in the game? Is it not the duty of the nation to protect its citizens from injuries against which no prudence or foresight on their part can shield them? Can it hope for the patriotic affection of those whom it does not protect? Is it not high time that the moral sense of the country was aroused on this subject? This nation can not afford to ignore the existence of a moral cancer so gigantic, knowing it to be a moral cancer. That it does know the immorality of gambling is proven by the manner in which it treats other forms of the evil that are far less harmful.

"Nor should the high social position, wealth or church connection of its votaries deter us from laying bare this iniquity, or the cry of pain that comes from the brown stone fronts stay the hand that holds the knife that is to rid the nation of this festering ulcer."

THE VALUE OF A TRADE JOURNAL'S DATA.

Long before the writer began the systematic investigation of the world's food supply he had become convinced that much of the so-called data, as to production and consumption, floating through the columns of the daily papers was either manufactured for a purpose or was of a fugitive character; originating no one knew where; without parentage; utterly valueless and misleading; but while somewhat distrustful of some of the tabular statements of the special trade journals—distrustful because of a lack of even apparent accord emanating from the same and variant sources—yet it was supposed that the conductors of reputable journals at least would exercise due care and diligence in procuring and tabulating reliable data, and in every case where official data was obtainable such alone would be used and every precaution taken to verify even official statements of which quantities and values formed a constituent part.

When a journal sets itself up as an instructor of the public and a purveyor of information, simple justice and honesty render it obligatory upon its conductors that they exercise the utmost care to not only secure all and the latest available data and information, but that it shall be of the highest possible character, and a journal failing to do this writes itself down a pretender and charlatan, securing attention and the money of its patrons by false and fraudulent pretenses. Such a journal is clearly entitled to neither confidence nor consideration at the hands of the people it has deceived and defrauded.

Busy men are unable to make original investigations, and rely upon specialists to do it and make publication in trade journals, and readily pay for such services—and the writer, like other busy men had, from its reputation, been led to accept the statements of the *Cincinnati Price Current* as reliable and trustworthy, although even in a hasty reading of that journal be discovered a lack of that complete accord with (its) prior utterances which should characterize the statements of every publication assuming so important a duty as that of furnishing producers, consumers, merchants, transporters and the general public with information and numerical data in relation to so vital a subject as that pertaining to the world's food supply and yet, such was the standing of the *Price Current* that the writer long deemed it but little short of heresy to question any of its statements, be they tabular or other, but being impelled, by the unprofitableness of his farming operations, to undertake an investigation of the present (and prospective) productive power of the fields of the temperate zones supplying the food of the bread eating world he soon found that neither the current statements or the tabulated data of the *Price Current* accorded with its previous utterances or with available official reports, many of its divergencies being so far out of line as to seem intentional, and it appeared to be in the habit of publishing any set of figures that would conform to the argument it desired to make. Careful reading of the *Price Current* brought the conviction home to the writer that a theory was first espoused and then figures adopted—if not manufactured—that would sustain the theory.

To make it clear that little or no reliance can be placed upon the statements and data published by the *Price Current*, a small part of the errors crowding its pages during recent weeks are instanced:

In its issue of July 9th the *Price Current* places the production of wheat in France in 1890 at 325,000,000 bushels and states the largest French crop during the past seven years to have been 325,000,000 and the smallest to have been 273,000,000 bushels, when it is officially stated, in the bulletins of the French Ministry of Agriculture for the years 1887, 1888 and 1889, and by the United States Department of Agriculture for 1884, 1885, 1886 and 1890, that the seven crops have given the following quantities:

1884 .... 324,130,000 bushels	1888.... .... 280,177,000 bushels
1885.............................. 312,912,000 "	1889 .... 307,357,000 "
1886....... .... 304,427,000 "	1890....... .... 338,902,000 "
1886.............................. 319,094,000 "	

From this official data, all of which was available in publications of the Department of Agriculture prior to the *Price Current's* issue of July 9th, we find that the largest French crop of the seven years was 13,902,000 bushels greater and the smallest crop of the series was 7,000,000 bushels greater than stated by the *Price Current*.

In the same issue it states that the Russian crop of 1890 was 197,000,000 bushels, the largest Russian crop of the seven years was 274,000,000 bushels and the smallest 178,000,-000, while the official figures show that the crop of 1890—exclusive of Poland—was 295 - 972,000 bushels, the largest crop 295,711,000 and the smallest 163,000,000 bushels, or a dif. ference, respectively, of 8,972,000 bushels, 21,711,000 bushels and 15,000,000.

In the same issue it tells us that the Italian wheat crop of 1890 was 126,000,000 bushels, the largest crop in seven years 129,000,000 bushels and the smallest one 103,000,-000 bushels. While this statement is but 640,000 bushels less than the official returns as to the crop of 1890, Bulletin No. 10 of the Italian Ministry of Agriculture shows that the largest crop during the seven years, other than that of 1890, was that of 1887, which gave the out-turn of 119,500,000 bushels, or 9,500,000 bushels less than the *Price Current's* largest crop, as that of 1890 was 2,360,000 bushels less; but the most singular thing about the *Price Current's* statements as to Italian wheat production is found in the fact that in its issue of July 23rd it places the average yearly production of wheat in Italy at 135,000,-000 bushels, being 6,000,000 bushels more than it states the greatest crop to have been. Is not the *Price Current* the only party that can make an average greater than the greatest number of the series going to make up such average?

When the *Price Current* published these astounding figures the official data relating to Italian crops, had long been available in the publications of the United States Department of Agriculture. And this so readily available data, and no doubt in the possession of the *Price Current* in the reports of the Department for April and June, 1891, shows that the average yield of the wheat fields of Italy during the last seven years to have been 113,480,000 bushels instead of the 135,000,000 stated by the *Price Current*.

The July 23d *Price Current* places the average production of wheat in Spain at 110,000,000 bushels while the data published by the Department of Agriculture, and which accords with that collated by the writer, makes the Spanish average 92,000,000 bushels for the decade and 87,779,000 bushels for the last seven years, the mean being some 20,000,000 bushels less than the *Price Current's* figures.

The *Price Current* makes the largest Spanish crop of the seven years 131,000,000 bushels while the official data shows it to have been but 113,500,000 bushels—a difference of 16,500,000 bushels—a mere trifle for this journal.

So carefully is the *Price Current* edited that in its issue of July 23d it states the average wheat crop of Hungary to be 125,000,000 bushels, and in the issue of July 9th it states the greatest Hungarian crop of the seven years to have been 165,000,000 bushels *and the smallest to have been* 194,000,000. Probably the *Price Current* is the first to make the discovery that 165 is more than 194, as it is probably the first to discover that a crop of 92,700,000 bushels can, by the use of an agile pen, be transposed into one of 194,000,000.

In the *Price Current* of July 23d the annual average production of wheat in Hungary is stated to be 40,000,000 bushels, and the smallest crop in the last seven years to have been 37,000,000 bushels, when the official reports show the average for the decade to have been 43,670,000 bushels, as they show the average during the last seven years to have been 46,000,000, while the smallest crop in seven is officially placed at 38,376,000 bushels; but then a matter of 1,375,000 bushels is of no consequence, especially when to be more exact necessitates reference to readily available official publications.

In the *Price Current's* issue of July 9th the smallest crop of the last seven, in Germany, is placed at 82,000,000 bushels, while official data readily available when such publication was made, shows that the smallest German crop, since 1883, gave an out-turn of ` 87,170,000, a difference of 5,170,000 bushels.

In the *Price Current* for July 23d it is in one place stated that the product of wheat in India, in 1891, was 255,435,000 bushels, while lower down in the same column the crop of 1890-91 is placed at an even 235,000,000, the difference being no less than 20,435,000. It is, however, but due to the *Price Current* to state that it now claims that the 235,000,000 bushel statement relates to the crop harvested in 1890, but such is not the reading of the statement in the issue of July 23d, and that such claim is an afterthought is made highly probable by the fact that in its issue of October 23d, 1890 it stated the product of the Indian harvest for that year at 225,000,000 bushels, being 10,000,000 bushels less than the out-turn it now sets up the claim that such crop gave.   Taking one horn of the dilemma there is an unexplained discrepancy in its statement of 20,435,000 bushels, while pendant from the other horn hangs a trifle of 10,000,000.

More than this; in its issue of July 23d there is tabulated the product of seven recent Indian wheat harvests, but the quantities of but two accord, even remotely, with the official figures thrice stated in (three of) the monthly reports of the Department of Agriculture.

In its issue of the 27th of August, the *Price Current* places the annual consumption of wheat and rye in France at *about* 405,000,000 bushels, while official data, available months, and part of it years, before such publication was made, shows that the production and *net* importation of wheat and rye—including a mixture of wheat and rye known as maslin—from 1887 to 1889, inclusive, to have been as follows:

YEARS.	Production, Bushels.	Net Importation Bushels.	Total Supply, Bushels.
1887-88	400,801,000	28,416,000	429,217,000
1888-89	355,579,000	47,768,000	403,347,000
1889-90	385,920,000	28,752,000	414,670,000
Totals............................	1,142,300,000	104,936,000	1,247,234,000
Averages......................................	380,766,000	34,979,000	415,745,000

It would appear that the *Price Current* understates the annual consumption of wheat and rye in France no less than 10,745,000 bushels, and this is made still more clear upon an examination of the reports of the U. S. Department of Agriculture for December, 1883, where it is shown that the consumption of wheat and rye (including mixtures of the two grains) for bread, seed and use in the arts during the ten years following the Franco-German war—when the population was fully a million less than now—averaged 406,000,000 bushels per year, being at the rate of 10.97 bushels per capita, while during the years tabulated above the per capita quota, for all purposes, has been 10.92 bushels. The quantity consumed is found to be a very constant one.

In the issue of the *Price Current* now under review it is stated that the United Kingdom will, during this cereal year, require to import 137,000,000 bushels of wheat, while the imports of the last four years are officially shown to have averaged more than 151,-000,000 bushels, and the British grain trade journals estimate the imports at from 152,000,000 to 165,000,000 bushels.

Moreover, the *Price Current* states the present annual consumption of Britain at about 210,000,000 bushels, when the production and net importation of wheat alone, during the last four years are found, from official reports, to have averaged more than 227,000,000 bushels (and about 2,500,000 bushels of rye) showing that the annual supply has exceeded the *Price Current's* statement by fully 17,000,000 bushels. At the time this reckless, misleading and wholly incorrect statement was sent out the official data, both as to production and importation, had long been readily available, showing the facts to be entirely at variance with *Price Current* utterances.

Every issue of the *Price Current* that the writer has examined carefully has been filled with errors of like character, but space permits but a small fraction to be enumerated, and the statement of one or two more must suffice.

In its issue of July 23d the *Price Current* states the annual average production of rye in Roumania to be 40,000,000 bushels and that of Italy to be 15,000,000. In its latest official out-givings the Roumanian government shows the rye acreage to be less than 430,000 acres and to produce 40,000,000 on such an area the yield must exceed 81 bushels per acre, and to produce crops averaging 15,000,000 bushels the rye fields of Italy must yield more than 38 bushels per acre.

Aside from the improbability of such yields when the *Price Current* sent forth such preposterous statements there was available, in the June report of the United States Department of Agriculture, the official report of the Italian Ministry showing that from 1884 to 1889, inclusive, the crops of rye had averaged but 4,084,000 bushels, while the July report of the Department, likewise available when this absurd publication was made, shows the yield of rye in Roumania in 1889 to have been 10,305.000 bushels.

When the attention of the *Price Current* was called to these very wide discrepancies, and it was asked to name its authority for such statements, the editor wrote:

"I do not find the data on which the compilation you refer to was based, as to Roumania, but *I think* this item was obtained from Beerbohm, while the figures for Italy *I think* were from a compilation which I published four or five years ago, from sources then deemed authentic, as an indication of average production *previous* to that time. I presume I may soon find this material and if it is different, especially with reference to Roumania, I will address you again."

This is an astounding confession coming, as it does, from the editor of a journal that poses as an authority upon so grave a subject as food production and consumption—a subject that involves the well being of nearly every man, woman and child in America. At best the *Price Current* is convicted, out of its own mouth, of imposing upon the public so-called data that has had no revision for years, for which it is unable to name any authority and, this too, when an abundance of official data was readily available.

It seems that the *Price Current* does not know where its figures came from, how they originated, and it has been shown that they not only vary from week to week but in the same issue and column.

Is not this one of the most bare-faced frauds that was ever perpetrated upon confiding patrons who are paying for this sort of stuff and relying upon it for the direction of their business?

The investigations of the writer show that much, if not all, the so-called data of this sheet is of this character, and the evidence furnished by the editor's confession, shows that instead of being derived, as it all should be, from available official sources the data used by the *Price Current* is raked from the gutter, taken from the scrap-heap or selected from the waste-basket.

Reading the *Price Current* in the bright light thrown upon it by this partial analysis of its statements and methods, and having such knowledge of the character of its so-called data as we thus obtain, the question at once presents itself:

What does this sheet now desire to prove? By whom and in what interest is it retained, and what is the amount of the retainer? Or is its mendacity and utter disregard of common honesty, in its dealings with its patrons, the logical result of infinite capacity for error and lack of ability?

Of what value are its deductions when the entire basis of the fabric is a matter of reckless guess work and fabrication?

EUROPEAN REQUIREMENTS AND PROBABLE SUPPLIES OF RYE AND WHEAT DURING THE 1891-92 CEREAL YEAR.

Requirements for bread......................	2,400,000,000	bushels
Requirements for seed....................................	300,000,000	"
Total requirements......................................	2,700,000,000	"
Probable out-turn of European fields ....1,800,000,000 bushels		
Seed required—a constant quantity................ 300 000,000 "		
Seven and one-half months' food supply.......... 1,500 000,000 "	1,800,000 000	"
Deficit equal to 4½ months' food supply...	900,000,000	"
America, India and all other countries can supply at outside...	280,000,000	"
Ultimate European deficit equal to three months' needs................	620,000,000	"

Potatoes and other substitutions may—possibly—be equal to half of one month's consumption, but this is not probable, as the potatoes are always consumed in addition to the wheat and rye; but admitting that such substitutions will equal half a month's consumption, how are the other two and a half months to be covered?

In Central Russia there are 18 provinces which the Kieff correspondent of the Liverpool *Corn Trade News*, for whose reliability the editor vouches in the strongest terms, after careful personal inspection, says have not harvested as much grain as was sown. These 18 provinces contain 39,000,000 inhabitants, and are not only the most populous but the most productive of the whole Empire, and largely constitute its granary. If these provinces have not grown the seed sown how are they to be fed? *The remainder of the Empire does not produce a surplus equal to the food requirements of 39,000,000 people.*

With Europe producing but seven and a half months' food and the outside world able to furnish but one and a half months' supply, would it not be good business policy for American farmers to

"HOLD THE WHEAT?"

GAMBLING IN FOOD PRODUCTS.

It may be true, as Mr. B. P. Hutchinson says in the *North American Review* for October, that all operations in the grains benefit the producer, but if he means, as would appear from the context, that such operations as constitute ninety-nine per cent. of the transactions upon the Boards of Trade then issue will be taken with this sweeping assertion by a vast number of conservative people aside from the producers, who are, practically, a unit in the belief that harm, and harm only, can result from such operations whether they temporarily advance or depress prices.

We are told that but for this form of speculation:

"The farmer could only sell his grain to local buyers, who would be liable to get full and stop buying, and then the farmer would be compelled to wait for customers; and in the meantime a mortgage might be foreclosed on his farm, even while the wheat in his bins would more than satisfy the mortgage if converted into cash."

The farmer objects not to speculation so much as to that sort of speculation of which Mr. Hutchinson might be termed "an instructive example."

The farmer does not, and probably never has, objected to that speculation which, when more grain was being marketed by the grower than was required by the consumer, impels the buying of grain as an investment, places it in a warehouse to await that time so sure to come when the volume of products being marketed by the grower shall be insufficient to meet current requirements, the result being, in the absence of the short-seller, such an advance in its value as to render the investment a remunerative one.

Prior to the evolution of the short-seller such speculative buying took the surplus grain which the farmer desired to sell and stored it for the consumer, a reasonable charge being made for the laudable service.

This may be termed speculation, but it is, as well, legitimate commerce, and is wholly different from that speculation which finds its province in the buying and selling of "options" and "puts and calls." The trouble with Mr. Hutchinson and the class which he represents is that they have no conception of commercial ethics and confound gambling with speculation and commerce, desiring us to believe that gambling is both moral and commendable, as well as necessary to the welfare of the community, and especially to that of the farmer, whom they represent as likely to fall into irretrievable ruin but for the kindly offices of the Board of Trade gambler, who puts prices up or down at will, and at times—as just after the Hutchinson wheat corner of 1888—renders it impossible to sell grain, in the country, at any price.

This fraternity is most solicitous lest the farmer shall be unable to sell his wheat and pay off a mortgage that otherwise might be foreclosed, but they seem to forget the old saying so long current, "good as wheat," and that in no part of the United States is it a very difficult matter to borrow money on wheat in the farm granary and that the one farmer in danger of having his farm sold under foreclosure is that one who has no wheat or but an unsufficient amount, in his granary.

It is possible that the farmer may have to wait for customers, but certainly not long while men continue to eat, and the speculator, be he of the laudable kind or of the short-selling variety, does not add anything to the number of consumers or hasten the consumption of the farmer's wheat by one minute, nor is it within his power to lessen the consumption, although the short-seller can, and doubtless does, lessen the price which the farmer receives by placing in competition quantities of fiat products which are as illimitable as are his greed and lack of commercial honesty.

Although the writer has probably not seen as many years as the advocate of gambling in food products, yet he has bought and sold much grain and has never seen a time —except at the end of some such gambling operation as that of September, 1888, upon which Mr. Hutchinson delights to expatiate—when grain was not readily salable, and prior to the time when modern methods of short-selling and running corners came into vogue prices were far more stable and fluctuations less destructive of legitimate profits. Until mankind is able to live without food the farmer will have a market for all he can produce, and instead of hereafter waiting for customers all the coming years are likely to see the consumer hurrying up the farmer and trying to hasten the marketing of crops that will rarely reach to the end of the harvest year.

Probably few men know better than Mr. Hutchinson that up to the time when short-selling became the means of determining prices the warehouses were filled with grain bought as an investment whereas now these warehouses stand less than one-third full the year through the capitalist being afraid to invest money in property the value of which may be so greatly lessened in a day, by the limitless offers of the short-seller, as to entail loss.

Thus has that kind of speculation, which is at best but the worst form of gambling, destroyed that laudable speculation which made a market for the products of the farm before they were needed by the consumer. Not only did this beneficient form of speculation go on at the trade centers but at every railway station and mill in the country absorbing and taking out of sight an enormous aggregate of farm products. Now, however, instead of buying grain to store the miller buys an "option" and if the price goes up collects the difference from the short-seller and goes into the market and buys the grain the day he desires to grind it his profit being found in the saving of waste, insurance, interest and storage room all of which accrue to the benefit of the miller or short-seller. In other words: in consideration of the deposit of a small margin by the miller the short-seller furnishes a vest-pocket elevator, insurance company, bank accommodations and a guarantee against waste—all of which operates against the farmer who must carry the grain and in case he requires money, while the price is lower than he believes it ought to be and will be, he must borrow from the banker.

While the short-selling speculator thus deprives him of the purchaser, for distant use, that he formerly enjoyed it is not the worst phase of the competition of the short-seller as the grain which the miller and investment buyer formerly took from off the market, and stored until needed for consumption, now all presses with fearful weight upon a market that is also loaded down by the daily *offering* of hundreds, and sometimes thousands of millions of fiat products.

The amount of grain required for current consumption is a constant quantity and more being *offered* than is required will necessarily depress the price, be it actual grain or simply the promises of the short-seller to deliver at some future day, and the volume of such *offerings* necessarily determines the price. If less than the current requirements prices are advanced by the buyer who has failed to secure the quantity his customers demand, while on the contrary if the quantity *offered* is largely in excess of current needs and there are no investing buyers of actual grain the price recedes. The world's yearly requirements of wheat and rye now approximate closely to 3,600,000,000 bushels, and, excluding Sundays and holidays, this implies daily needs of 12,000,000 bushels; hence we may assume that if the *offerings* for any considerable period exceed the sum of the daily requirements the effect will be to lessen prices, and so long as the *offerings* continue to be greater than the consumption so long will the tendency of prices be downward and no advance in price can be expected, no matter what the probabilities as to the future supply may be, until the pinch of scarcity shows that the *offerings* of the short-seller are but emanations from the lungs of a horde of unprincipled gamblers. So long, however, as the actual deliveries of the farmer exceed or equal the world's requirements and these *offerings* of fiat products continue and there are no investment buyers of the farmer's surplus there can be no permanent advance.

It goes without saying that so long as these conditions obtain and so long as more fiat grain is *offered* upon the markets of the world, by these industrious producers of "promises to deliver," so long must the farmer expect low prices, and instead of being a benefit to the producer this kind of speculation—which has certainly slaughtered all investment buying of grain—is the greatest curse that could be inflicted upon any community by a horde of gamblers who are under the protection of the law, and who plume themselves upon their ability to run wheat up to two dollars a bushel; advance the price of the loaf and make the "other fellow" settle his bets at a price which the successful worker of the corner fixes at twice the sum the farmer receives for the product of the fields upon which his labor has been expended and in which he has invested a vast capital.

When a successful corner has been made possible because there happens to be but

3,830,000 bushels of the "contract grade" of wheat that could be got to market within the month—September 1888—(although the country was full of wheat of lower grade that would make good bread) the worker of the corner, by paying two dollars a bushel for one or more car-loads of the contract grade, fixes the price at which he will settle with those who are "short to him"—mind you the last thing that he desires is that they shall be able to deliver the grain which he has contracted to receive yet never expected or intended to receive, and had the "shorts" been able to have delivered a few hundred thousand bushels more no doubt the corner would have been broken and the cornerer bankrupted instead of the shorts, although he might still have plumed himself with having advanced the price of the loaf of which, however, there is no proof.

Expatiating upon the benefits of this kind of speculation to the producer Mr. Hutchinson neglects to inform the reader that immediately he had settled with the "shorts" upon their contracts, to deliver grain, that would certainly have ruined him if complied with, the price of wheat dropped back to about what it was when he started to work the corner and that many of the short sellers had been stripped, by such settlement, as bare as when they came into the world, and the business of the country h . . been disturbed that one man might have "gain without merit."

Is it not illogical to say that when wheat is too cheap the selling of "options" and "puts and calls" aids the producer and in the next breath tell us that:

"Grain operations benefit the consumer also; because when there is an excess of bread-stuffs, a low price stimulates consumption and gives a big loaf and when there is a deficit a high price enforces economy and teaches him to eat more potatoes and esculent roots and less bread and thus give his neighbor a chance at the loaf?"

It is somewhat difficult to understand how speculation can add to one's appetite and stimulate consumption. Is it a fact, that here, where all but those in extreme indigence are always fully fed, that a low price stimulates consumption of the cheapest form of food? Have not our people at all times all the bread they are able to consume? Is it not known to every school boy that bread is, by far, the cheapest form of food when nutritive properties are considered?

While we were long since told that "man shall not live by bread alone" it still remains the one constant factor in the diet of the bread-eating people and being the cheap est form in which the masses can readily obtain the required nutriment is the last to be dispensed with, and the quantity eaten is lessened in but a slight degree by an advance in price. When flour was selling at $15 per barrel, during the Crimean war, there is no evidence that consumption was materially lessened either in this country or Western Europe.

Few will question the benefits derived from the use of capital in dealing with food products, but it is not the capital of the pernicious short-seller which performs the laudable service of distribution.

While nothing could be more remote from the desire of the writer than to belittle the services of capital actually employed in distribution, it is his desire to call attention to the fact that what is known as the visible supply of grain, during the last ten years, has averaged under 30,000,000 bushels of wheat, less than 10,000,000 bushels of corn and some 5,000,000 bushels of oats, with small quantities of rye and barley, all aggregating some 46,000,000 bushels and worth less than $40,000,000 and it is quite safe to say that adding the value of all the crude food and fiber products in transit, in mill, warehouse and factory, as well as the value of the plants used in their distribution, the entire sum would at no time exceed $500,000,000. On the other hand the farmer, who is never thought of as a capitalist, has invested in his land and its equipment for production a sum that probably exceeds $16,000,000,000 and as he carries an average of half the year's crop for the entire period his further investment is over $700,000,000 and in this form alone greatly exceeds the entire investment of all those directly engaged in the distribution of his products.

I trust that the short-selling gamblers of the Boards of Trade will pardon the suggestion that the farmer could get on much better without their aid than can the real capitalist, engaged in distribution, get on without the farmer, who is not called upon to be specially grateful for the use of such sums as the distributors use in the furtherance of their business.

Would it not be well if other members of the community should recognize the fact that the farmer employes a vast capital in his business? Would it not also be well if the fact was more generally recognized that when the capital of the farmer is unprofitably employed, by reason of inadequate prices for his products, every interest suffers and stagnation pervades the economic fabric?

It is beyond controversy that the prosperity of the nation, as a whole, waits upon the prosperity of that forty per cent., more or less, that inhabits the farm. Yet, there seems a tacit combination of others to prevent the farmer from getting such a price for his products as their cost and supply and demand now justify and when it appears that the farmer is likely to secure such a return as will afford him something more than the meager subsistence which has, of late, been his only reward, the grain gambler, the transporter, merchant and banker rush into print and tell us that if we insist upon such prices as will afford a fair return for the services of the farmer we shall scare away the starving customer from Europe who can find supplies no where else on earth and others will take possession of markets that we alone have the means of supplying. So great is the solicitude lest the farmer shall secure something near what the worker of the wheat corner, of September, 1888, was able to squeeze out of the "shorts", as the value of the bushel of wheat which they failed to deliver upon their gambling contracts, that there is held up to our horrified gaze the poor Russian who is likely to loose his hold upon the markets of Western Europe because the Tzar has found it necessary to prohibit the exportation of rye lest the 50,000,000 people inhabiting the stricken provinces should perish.

Another "bugaboo" which the venerable dealer in "puts and calls" holds up to frighten the farmer from ruining the export market by insisting upon the fair price for his products which the scant supply warrants is that the Scandinavian peasant, whom we are told now eats bread made from half tree bark and half flour, will add another twenty-five per cent. of this most nutritious substance and deprive the American wheat-grower of a market! Since when have Swedes, Norwegians and Danes taken to a bark diet? What is its nutritive value? What is the tree which furnishes this edible substance? Does it produce annual crops of edible bark and will it thrive in America?

Does not our speculative friend know that while Scandinavia yearly imports some 2,500,000 bushels of wheat and about 12,000,000 bushels of rye that Scandinavian exports of other cereals exceed such quantities by some 6,000,000 bushels?

Does it not approach the ridiculous to even suggest that the Tzar hazards the market for Russian grain in trying to save the lives of his starving subjects by retaining a crop of rye that, added to all the wheat that has been harvested, is officially found to be less than the ordinary requirements of the Russian people by more than a hundred million bushels?

The essayist informs us that he "has studied this subject—presumably that of the world's food supply, as well as short-selling—closely and for a long time." He has certainly studied it to little purpose if he has not learned that with average crops upon so much of its surface as the world has thus far been able to devote to the production of rye and wheat that the annual product is now less than the world's annual requirements by hundreds of millions of bushels and that the annual deficit is increasing at the rate of more than 30,000,000 bushels per year, and that the reason the pinch of scarcity has not sooner been felt was to be found in the existence of great reserves heaped up in the years, prior to 1886, when the world's wheat area (and production) was in excess of current requirements.

Is it possible that the essayist is ignorant of the fact that while the bread-eaters of the world have, since 1885, increased fully 33,000,000 and the requirements of wheat and rye augmented by more than 230,000,000 bushels—equal to the product of more than 19,000,000 average acres—the wheat and rye acreage of the world has increased barely 2,000,000 acres and but for the drafts which the world was able to make upon reserve stores the bread-eaters of many lands would long since have known the pinching scarcity which implies high prices?

It would appear impossible that after such long and close study the essayist should be ignorant of the fact that during the ninth decade the wheat and rye area of the world increased but 1.4 per cent. as against an increase in the wheat and rye eating population of no less than 14 per cent.

Because the people of America have not been called upon to supply any considerable part of the rye required by the people of Europe the short-selling fraternity either forget or are ignorant of the fact that when rye is scarce wheat must very largely take its place, and that the scarcity of one necessarily affects the demand and price for the other, as they seem to be ignorant of the fact that in dealing with the world's supply of breadstuffs they must be treated as one in order to measure the world's needs with any degree of accuracy.

While the essayist tells us that in consequence of the Tzar's proclamation Russia is likely to "have an unsold surplus and have lost valuable customers," does he not know that a famishing man will not put seed in the ground that he needs to prevent immediate starvation, and that such is to-day the condition of a great part of Russia, and that the press is now teeming with the information that the sowings, in the famine stricken provinces, are thus being greatly curtailed, as I said they were likely to be as long ago as early in June?

There are those who anticipate a greatly reduced out-turn from Russian fields during the near-by years as the result of the present dearth of seed, the loss of great numbers of work animals, and the starvation or dispersion of no inconsiderable number of the cultivators.

If such anticipations are realized only in part it will be years before Russia need mourn the loss of customers, whose places, however, are likely to be taken by those whom we now supply, but which Mr. Hutchinson agrees with me in saying must give place to "the immense population that will occupy, before many years, the territory between the Mississippi and the Atlantic."

To convince us that we should let the short-seller determine the price for our products in such a way as not to scare away our customers we are told that:

"We might if excessively greedy for money, drive the consumers to using substitutes, and that would be bad for both sides. In the interior of Cuba, San Domingo and Brazil the poorer classes never see bread at all."

While this is doubtless very interesting and instructive, it is difficult to see what is the value, as customers of the wheat grower, of people who never see bread, and it seems quite safe to say, judging from what we know of periods of scarcity in the past, that so long as people can secure the means of purchase they will continue to eat bread, as did the people of Britain in 1801 when wheat sold for $5.40 per bushel, and when, as during the first twenty years of this century, the English loaf was made from wheat that cost, on an average of $2.60 per bushel, the price of the quartern loaf once rising to forty-seven cents although it has recently sold for less than ten cents while wages, of the English artisan and laborer, are now much higher than in the earlier decades of the century.

Even when wheat was selling at $5.40 per bushel the poor would not substitute the Indian rice upon which, as a measure of relief, the government had thrown away a bounty, to induce importation, of no less than $1,700,000 preferring to buy the high priced wheat.

By the way, does it not appear a little singular that Mr Hutchinson did not discover when he put wheat up to two dollars a bushel in 1888 that "it would be bad for both sides"? That, however, being mostly wind wheat, he probably felt justified in acting upon the theory that as it could not be eaten the consumer would not be affected although he likes to say that it did enhance the price of the poor man's loaf.

The history of the entire past shows quite conclusively that the last thing to be dispensed with is bread. If an economy in food becomes necessary such articles of diet as are either less nutritive or more costly will first be dispensed with and it may not be amiss to remind the short-sellers that when the necessity for substitution arises the substitutes are usually not obtainable in sufficient volume to afford much relief and the very fact of the substitution of a less desirable article for one to which the consumer has always been accustomed and for which he has a great preference implies quite as high prices as the producer of the scarce article is likely to desire.

When the crops of wheat and rye are greatly deficient it is not unusual for the other crops to be meager and those who talk so glibly of substitutions seems to have lost sight of the fact that such things as potatoes, other grains, and all possible substitutes but tree bark, are rarely produced in excess of current needs and are all consumed in addition to the wheat and rye even in years of average yield of all food crops. This year of deficient production of rye and wheat proves to be no exception in this respect, as in the devastated districts of Russia other crops are nearly or quite as deficient as those of the bread-making grains, and the potato crop is as complete a failure as it is possible for mind to conceive, while that of hay is little if any better, and the pastures have been sere and brown the year through, the result being that the farmer can neither sell nor feed his animals, as no one has forage.

That potatoes cannot, this year, be substituted for the deficient grains, over the most of Central and Western Europe, is made certain by the character of a potato crop which is nowhere above an average and over vast areas is greatly below rendering it clear that the quantity harvested will be below the amount ordinarily consumed and indicating the desirability of even finding some substitute, other than tree bark, for the deficient potatoes.

In Europe, as a whole, other roots are a deficient crop, and this is especially true of wide areas in Britain, while there is fear of great distress in Ireland because of potato blight.

In France a large part of the frost-ravaged wheat fields were resown to oats, the crop of which is some 15 per cent. above the average, and in France oats are not unlikely to be substituted, in part, for wheat and rye, both of which are greatly deficient in quantity and even more so as to quality, some recent estimates putting the wheat fit for milling as low as 50 per cent. of a yield estimated to aggregate not more than 64 per cent. of an average, while in no case is the grain up to the standard in either weight or nutritive power.

Thomas Tooke, in his work on prices, lays it down as an axiom that "a very small deficiency in the case of necessaries will cause a very great increase in the price: e. g., that wheat may rise from 100 to 300 per cent. when the deficiency in the crops is not more than 15 or 30."

The writer estimates the wheat and rye crops of the world, just harvested, to be from 18 to 20 per cent. below an average, and by reason of an acreage deficient for some years the aggregate product to be 20 per cent. below the world's requirements. The reader can readily make the application of Tooke's law.

Mr. Hutchinson tells us we supply Europe because we have a new soil, plenty of acres and use implements that cheapen production, and that a dollar a bushel for wheat at Minneapolis means a great deal for such a farmer as Oliver Dalrymple who is represented as saying "that his wheat cost him about thirty cents a bushel with a good yield."

How many farmers are there in the world who grow wheat under as favorable conditions as Mr. Dalrymple? Does not even two per cent. on all their investments mean much to such capitalists as a Vanderbilt or an Astor while meaning very little to the widow whose whole fortune is but five thousand dollars?

Mr. Hutchinson forgets to tell us how often Mr. Dalrymple secures the "good yield" which enables him to produce wheat at *about* thirty cents a bushel, but the intention seems to be that the impression should go abroad that to produce wheat upon our western farms it costs but thirty cents per bushel, and that a dollar for it at the great markets means that the farmer will roll in wealth and vie with the railroad magnate in his expenditures, hence the insistence upon a fair price for his grain is all wrong.

While it is within the possible that some of Mr. Dalrymple's crops may have been produced at a cost as low as thirty cents, yet I venture the suggestion that such sum does not begin to represent the average cost of the crops he has grown during the last five years, as I know that twice that sum does not begin to cover the cost of growing wheat upon lands, that even in this new country, require considerable expenditures for fertilization, and it is both unjust to the farmer, and misleading, to put forward such a statement, as the cost of production, which it is quite safe to assume, averages much nearer a dollar and still leaves little as a return for the capital invested.

Were it otherwise, would not western farmers be more prosperous, and would so many of the farms be subject to foreclosure were the short-seller to be prevented from making a market for wheat?

If wheat could be profitably grown at twice thirty cents it is safe to say that but few farms would be in danger of being sold under foreclosure. The low price of wheat—wheat being the key to the aggricultural situation—no matter how brought about, has been the primary cause of the continued existence of American farm mortgages, as it has been of the bankruptcy of so many of the tenant farmers of Britain, and it is the effect of short-selling to continue these low prices, when the conditions of supply warrant high ones, that constitute the burthen of the farmer's objection to that form of speculation for which Mr. Hutchinson appears as the advocate, and which, in practice, assumes the worst possible form of gambling, as the losses ultimately all fall upon the farmer who takes no voluntary part in the game, is its most unwilling victim, and is never permitted to share in the winnings.

We are told by Mr. Hutchinson that: "South America will have from the Argentine Republic a surplus of perhaps 30,000,000 bushels."

Is it not strange that after such "long and close study" of this subject Mr. Hutchinson should so presume upon the credulity or ignorance of the public as to put forth such a statement when reference to the Consular report for April, 1890, page 610, shows the exports of wheat from Argentina to have been 8,730,000 bushels in 1887, 6,560,000 bushels in 1888 and but 840,000 bushels in 1889, the aggregate for the three years being but little more than half that thirty million bushels that the public is now told we may expect from a crop that has yet to pass the critical period of its growth and which covers but about 3,000,000 acres? Was this statement, that is a third greater than the entire exports of the last four years, put forward in ignorance or for the purpose of misleading the public?

The whole short-selling fraternity constantly exagerate the extent of the crops and the exportable surplus of the wheat growing countries and then base upon such exaggerations an argument for low prices, and they are now engaged in sending abroad statements that although we have exported 60,000,000 bushels from this crop we still have an exportable surplus remaining of from 200,000,000 to 250,000,000 bushels and can supply all the needs of Europe without difficulty and shall have an unmarketable surplus left upon our hands if we do not hurry our grain to market at a low price.

A favorite argument of the short-seller is that there is a harvest somewhere in the world every month in the year, hence there can be no enduring scarcity. This is not true so far as relates to commercial crops of the bread-making grains, and these instructors of the public neglect to tell us that the entire exportable surplus of wheat of the southern hemisphere would barely furnish Europe with bread for three days, and that the cultivated area of that hemisphere, outside the tropics, is less than that of the one State of Illinois.

The short-seller makes the claim that his sales do not and cannot affect the price for farm products, as the seller implies the buyer. While this may be nominally true where actual sales of even options are made there are an immense number of "wash-sales" constantly being made for the purpose of breaking down prices that the short-seller may buy in his outstanding contracts at a profit, and when the great short-sellers enter into a combination, as they often do, to "bear" prices they usually effect their object and the lower prices are hammered, and the less buying the greater are their *offerings*, and it is these *offerings* that determines the price which the farmer is forced to accept for his products, and thus is he most directly affected by all these operations.

That these operations, while making the price for the products of the farm, are fictitious and but gambling devices is made most clear by the fact that delivery of property but in rare instances follows the making of these hundreds of thousands of contracts to deliver. *For instance, at the close of the September, 1891, deals, during which month thou-*

sands of millions of bushels of wheat and corn were contracted to be delivered at Chicago by the short-sellers, the actual deliveries at the maturity of these contracts were less than 50,000 bushels of wheat and 35,000 bushels of corn, the other "deals" having been settled by payment of the difference which constituted the winnings of the fortunate gamblers.

Does not Mr. Hutchinson know that when by such operations the price of wheat has been reduced to the extent of one cent a bushel it means much to farmers other than Mr. Dalrymple, and that upon an average wheat crop it amounts to no less than a loss of $4,500,000 to the producer?

Mr. Hutchinson informs us that among the brightest of the great millers who have placed Minneapolis at the head of the milling world is Mr. Charles A. Pillsbury, but he is careful not to inform his readers what are the opinions of this the greatest dealer in the world in actual farm products as to the practice of short-selling, as set forth on pages 65 and 70 ante.

The Cincinnati *Price Current* says:

"Here is the evil—the sale of wind *contracts*, inflated by the margin system, having the same power of influencing values that an equal *offering* of actual property would have."

Mr. Denison B. Smith, Secretary of the Toledo Board of Trade, says:

"We most heartily deprecate the conditions prevailing in this country. First is the apparent want of courage on the part of capitalists to invest in wheat, and the next is the reckless disposition of the fraternity of short-sellers to pound down prices. Not an advance in prices has occurred on this side that has not been reflected abroad, and not a decline that has not been followed by a corresponding break over there."

The first of Mr. Smith's conditions is the inevitable corollary of the second, and the capitalist will recover his courage and invest in wheat the moment the short-seller is taxed out of existence.

This evil has now invaded the markets of Britain, and in the Liverpool correspondence of *Dornbusch* of September 5th, 1891, it is stated that:

"Our local market is dominated by a crowd of dealers in 'options' and 'futures,' putting prices up and down every ten minutes, and with a similar state of things in America it is difficult to know where we are."

About May 1st, Leopold Bloom retired from the Chicago wheat pit worth "a clean million dollars" and was reported in the Chicago Tribune as giving his reasons for retiring in the following language:

"It's too much of a strain on a man to stand for any length of time without wearing out. One is under pressure all the time. He is betting his money against the market. If he buys and she goes up he is a winner. If she goes down he is a loser. It's a plain case of gamble, but it's legal and faro isn't. If they would take the limit off faro it would be a better game than wheat, because you could get quicker action but with the limit on there isn't money enough in it."

Mr Bloom is much more frank in rightly characterising the game than are most of its devotees who appear to be ashamed of its real character.

Shall twenty thousand short-sellers be longer permitted to bring the product of their lungs (which costs nothing) into destructive competition with the useful and costly products of the world's many millions of farms in which is invested more than $100,000,000?

The conscience of the nation has decreed the suppression of the Louisiana lottery that is far less immoral than short selling and inflicts harm only upon those voluntarily becoming its victims.

Must the great industrial hosts of the farm suffer that a mere squad (comparatively) of worthless, short-selling gamblers may continue to bet upon prices and secure "gain without merit?"

THE FOLLOWING TABLE

Shows the Average Annual Product of Rye and Wheat, the Estimated Requirements, and the Out-turn promised by the harvest of 1891.

	Annual average product of Rye and Wheat 1881 to 1890	Requirements of Rye and Wheat for the 1891-2 cereal year	Estimated out-turn of Rye and Wheat harvest of 1891
France	385,000,000	416,000,000	274,000,000
Russia, Poland and Finland	960,000,000	800,000,000	590,000,000
Austria-Hungary	282,000,000	266,000,000	250,000,000
Germany	313,000,000	377,000,000	242,000,000
Italy	122,000,000	150,000,000	120,000,000
Spain	121,000,000	130,000,000	104,000,000
United Kingdom	61,000,000	236,000,000	70,000,000
Roumania	46,000,000	30,000,000	46,000,000
Turkey, Bulgaria and Roumelia	51,000,000	44,000,000	51,000,000
Belgium	38,000,000	66,000,000	26,000,000
Netherlands	18,000,000	36,000,000	16,000,000
Switzerland	8,000,000	21,000,000	7,000,000
Portugal, Greece, Servia and Scandinavia	76,000,000	106,000,000	70,000,000
North America	502,000,000	426,000,000	591,000,000
South America	31,000,000	40,000,000	44,000,000
Australasia	35,000,000	32,000,000	39,000,000
India	253,000,000	226,000,000	255,000,000
Other Countries	120,000,000	130,000,000	120,000,000
World Totals	**3,442,000,000**	**3,534,000,000**	**2,916,000,000**

An apparent world deficit of 18 per cent. or 619,000,000 bushels.

It should be remembered that rye forms thirty-eight per cent. of the two great bread-making grains and that of the bread eaten in Europe it constitutes no less than forty-seven per cent., and that in dealing with the requirements of the world, rye and wheat can not be separated.

There can be no doubt that the London *News* is correct when it says that American farmers are the masters of the situation, and can fix their own price for the great crop now being harvested.

ERRATA.

Page 10—Second line from top should read "short of bread-stuffs."
Page 17—At close of last line substitute for "in or" "or in other cases."
Page 19—First line should read "is likely to become."
Page 19—Third line of second paragraph should read "necessaries of life."
Page 35—Fourth line of third paragraph should read "great markets."
Page 35—Fourth and fifth paragraphs should be read as one.
Page 54—Fifth word of fourth paragraph is "cut."